STUDY GUIDE

Foundations

An Overview of Systematic Theology

R.C. Sproul

LIGONIER MINISTRIES
Renew your Mind.
LIGONIER.ORG | 800-435-4343

421 Ligonier Court, Sanford, FL 32771
Email: info@ligonier.org

Printed in China.

1

What Is Theology?

INTRODUCTION

There is much confusion behind the word *theology*. While most disciplines such as biology or zoology are commonly understood, the study of God is usually a foreign concept. In this lesson, Dr. Sproul defines the term *theology* as a subject that encompasses all of what God has revealed generally and specially.

MESSAGE OVERVIEW

I. What is systematic theology?
  a. The word *theology* can be understood by dividing it into *theos* and *logos*. *Logos* means "word" or "reason" and *theos* means "God." Theology concerns the application of logic to God.
  b. Dr. Sproul spoke at a college and lectured to the faculty on the topic, "What is a Christian college?" On his tour of the campus, he noticed a revealing inscription. The study of theology, not the study of religion, is at the heart of what makes a Christian education.

II. What are some aversions to systematic theology?
  a. The word *systematic* is often very negative to people. Most are not biased against mechanical systems, but the idea of a systematic way of understanding reality has been opposed by several ideologies.
  b. As people try to squeeze biblical ideas into preconceived, anti-biblical systems, it is no wonder the Bible does not appear coherent.
    i. Existentialism
    ii. Relativism

III. What is the nature of biblical revelation?
  a. Biblical revelation is the Word of God. It has diversity, but within it there is order.

i. Unity
ii. Coherence
iii. Consistency

b. The systematic theologian depends upon the biblical scholar, for theology is rooted in the details of Scripture.
c. Every detail of theology has an impact on every other detail of it.

STUDY QUESTIONS

1. What is the definition of theology?
   a. The study of Christ
   b. The study of the revelation of God
   c. The study of God Himself
   d. The study of the Holy Spirit

2. What is the reason Dr. Sproul gives for why we should study theology specifically?
   a. Theology is the light by which we see all the sciences.
   b. Theology is the queen of the sciences and needs to be returned to her rightful place of honor.
   c. Theology better equips the student to glorify God and to enjoy Him forever.
   d. Theology better captures what religion departments need to be teaching college students.

3. What is the goal of systematic theology?
   a. To place the Bible into a pre-existing system of thought
   b. To see how the Bible naturally fits together into an organized whole
   c. To trace a particular theme throughout the Bible and to see where it leads
   d. To see what the church has said about the Bible in times past

4. The idea of systematic theology is based on several assumptions. Which of the following was *not* mentioned by Dr. Sproul as one of those assumptions?
   a. God has revealed Himself in His Word.
   b. The word of God is living and active.
   c. God is not the author of chaos; His Word is coherent.
   d. The Word of God is rationally consistent.

5. Which philosophy has done the most harm to the study of systematic theology?
   a. Rationalism
   b. Empiricism
   c. Relativism
   d. Existentialism

6. When God speaks coherently, every detail that He says has an impact on every other detail He reveals to us.
   a. True
   b. False

DISCUSSION QUESTIONS

1. What is systematic theology?

2. Why is theology distasteful to many people? Tell of any experiences you may have had with people who were opposed to “anything but the Bible.”

3. What is the nature of biblical revelation?

4. What questions do you hope this series will answer about systematic theology?

2

Scope and Purpose of Theology

INTRODUCTION

Why do we continue to study theology even after many learned scholars have developed comprehensive systems of thought? In this lesson, Dr. Sproul explains that the scope and purpose of our study of theology is ultimately to be instructed by God and to grow in obedience to Him.

MESSAGE OVERVIEW

I. "Bringing the Light of the Reformation to Scripture"
   - The phrase on the cover of the New Geneva Study Bible is an example of what we *don't* mean to communicate about theology—that we bring an external system to the Bible and intentionally interpret it through that grid.

II. Theology is a science that attempts to gain a consistent knowledge of God.
   a. A paradigm shift is a radical shift in the operating principles of a science.
   b. An anomaly is an exception to a paradigm, but when anomalies build up, a paradigm shift eventually will occur. A new model must be constructed to make sense of the new information and experiences.
   c. What would a paradigm shift in theology look like? Why would it come? We have had the same basic data for two thousand years. But shifts are driven by new philosophies and societal changes, as people desire to view the data differently.
      i. Progress in theology
      ii. Non-progress in theology

III. There are three spheres of theology.
   a. Biblical theology is concerned with going through the Bible and studying all the verbiage on a given topic. The biblical theologian looks at the data, not the his-

tory or systems of thought. Biblical theology has been corrupted by "atomism," which leads to isolating biblical ideas, claiming that different writers of Scripture had radically different theologies and understandings of God.

b. Historical theology is a study of the history of theological development. Much can be derived from this study, especially when we meet "new" doctrines that have in fact been dealt with hundreds of years previously. Knowing historical theology is one key to remaining orthodox as you search the Scriptures.

c. Systematic theology is done when commentators teach how to interpret the whole scope of Scripture. The systematic theologian relies on the previously mentioned branches of theology.

IV. What is the value or purpose of Theology?

a. Everyone is a theologian, even those who deny it with every breath.

b. Second Timothy 3:16 is the biblical response to those who deny the importance of theology.

i. Doctrine

ii. Reproof

iii. Instruction in righteousness

STUDY QUESTIONS

1. What new information is being introduced into the study of theology?
   a. A better understanding of the biblical languages
   b. A better synthesis between modern philosophy and the ancient religion
   c. A better technique for introducing insights into the text
   d. A better model for accounting for the anomalies in the biblical text

2. The word *science* comes from the Latin word meaning what?
   a. Wisdom
   b. Knowledge
   c. Understanding
   d. Logic

3. Which of the following does Dr. Sproul *not* mention as one of the three spheres of theology?
   a. Systematic theology
   b. Practical theology
   c. Historical theology
   d. Biblical theology

4. Why should the study of theology be unavoidable for the Christian?
   a. Because the Christian should want to know God more
   b. Because the Christian should want to grow in wisdom and knowledge
   c. Because the Christian should want to practice good works
   d. Because the Christian should want to speak accurately about their Lord

5. What is the chief and principal source for the study of systematic theology?
   a. The Bible
   b. Church history
   c. Creeds and Confessions
   d. Reformed theology

6. Which system of biblical interpretation has been devastating to the Christian faith in recent years?
   a. Antinomianism
   b. Legalism
   c. Literalism
   d. Atomism

DISCUSSION QUESTIONS

1. What is the problem with the phrase "Bringing the Light of the Reformation to Scripture"?

2. What is an example of a paradigm shift in science? What is the cause of such a shift in theology? How does creativity play a part in theology?

3. What are the three spheres of theology? How do they interact?

4. What is the value or purpose of theology? Is it rooted in the Bible?

3

General Revelation and Natural Theology

INTRODUCTION

While Scripture is the supreme source of revelation concerning God, it is not the only source. The Bible tells us that we can clearly see God's eternal power and divine nature in the created realm. In this lesson, Dr. Sproul affirms the biblical truth that general revelation and natural theology are sufficient to leave all people without excuse.

MESSAGE OVERVIEW

I. Christianity is not based on speculation; it is a revealed faith.
   a. The truth we embrace has come from God. We call this revelation.
   b. General revelation and special revelation are the two sources of information we have about God. God is the source of all truth, whether "spiritual" or not.
      i. Illustration of a fountain head
      ii. St. Augustine's illustration of vision
      iii. Objections from a modern scientist
   c. General revelation goes to all the world. Psalm 19:1 is the biblical proof for this. Interior knowledge of God is taught in Romans 1. General revelation is not in the Bible. It is God's revelation of Himself through nature. It is also general because of its content. It is not specific, not strictly "law" or "Gospel."
   d. Natural revelation is usually a synonym for general revelation. But there is another category that is often confused with general revelation.

II. Natural theology can be distinguished from general revelation.
   a. Between God and man is nature. Through the medium of nature, God communicates about Himself. This is something God does to reveal Himself to us.

  b. Does that revelation that God gives ever get into our minds? How much do we miss? Natural theology is the result of what God does, of what God reveals, of what gets into our minds.
  c. There have been opponents of natural theology in the church. But Romans 1 seems to indicate that we do have a limited, non-salvific knowledge of God. On the other hand, Paul says that in Corinthians natural man cannot know God. Which is right?
    i. The verb "to know" is used in different ways.
    ii. Example: Old Testament references to "knowing" people
    iii. Romans 1:18–20—God is concerned about what people do with the information He gives to them, so they must know something. Verse 21 says they know God but refuse to obey.
    iv. We know God in one sense, but in another, natural man does not know Him. Natural theology is distorted by our sin, but general revelation is perfectly revealed.

STUDY QUESTIONS

1. What are the two kinds of general revelation mentioned in this lesson?
   a. Creation without; conscience within
   b. The Bible without; the Spirit within
   c. The Bible without; conscience within
   d. Creation without; the Spirit within

2. What is the means by which we can know truth?
   a. Philosophy
   b. Revelation
   c. Religion
   d. Experience

3. What other discipline should we be careful not to confuse with natural revelation?
   a. Progressive theology
   b. Natural theology
   c. Spiritual theology
   d. Open theology

4. General revelation is perfect in its execution, but why is natural theology distorted in its study?
   a. Because men do not know there is a God
   b. Because men, in their sinfulness, suppress the truth about God
   c. Because not every man has been given the Holy Spirit
   d. Because natural theology shouldn't be a discipline

5. Christianity stands or falls as a revealed faith.
   a. True
   b. False

6. What Latin term is used to describe the plainness of God's natural revelation in Romans 1:19?
   a. *Orsprong*
   b. *Manifestum*
   c. *Phaneros*
   d. *Yada*

DISCUSSION QUESTIONS

1. How are special revelation and natural/general revelation different?

2. Natural theology is how man perceives general revelation. How is natural theology distorted?

3. In what sense do we know and not know God through general revelation?

4. What is the problem with God judging people if general revelation is not perfect?

4

Special Revelation

INTRODUCTION

While God has revealed Himself to us in creation, the knowledge necessary for salvation is revealed to us only in Scripture. In this lesson, Dr. Sproul maintains that God has given us direct revelation of Himself through sacred Scripture and that Jesus Christ is the fullness of His revelation.

MESSAGE OVERVIEW

I. General revelation has several aspects.
   a. General revelation has divisions we have already discussed, but there are other important ones.
      i. Mediate: Revelation given by God through a medium other than Himself (Rom. 1)
      ii. Immediate: Revelation planted inside us by God, not gleaned via a medium (Rom. 2)

II. Special revelation is received through Scripture, and only occasionally have men received special revelation any other way.
   a. Hebrews 1 is a good example of this kind of revelation.
   b. Philosophers have debated the role reason and the senses play in receiving data. But regardless of our resolution of this debate, special revelation is knowledge derived directly from God with the highest possible certitude.
   c. This revelation has not always been through Scripture.
      i. Dreams, visions, Urim and Thummim
      ii. Theophany: An outward manifestation of the invisible God; for instance, the burning bush (Ex. 3)
      iii. Inspiration

   d. Three tests for true and false prophets: commission from God, presence of miracles, fulfillment of announcements

III. Hebrews 1 tells us of the supreme revelation of God to us.
   a. Jesus is the ultimate revelation of God to us.
   b. In the Upper Room, Jesus says that "he who has seen Me has seen the Father."

STUDY QUESTIONS

1. What type of revelation is Scripture?
   a. Mediate revelation
   b. Immediate revelation
   c. Mediator revelation
   d. Medium revelation

2. What did Dr. Sproul say was perhaps the most famous theophany in Scripture?
   a. The burning pot revealed to Abraham
   b. The burning bush revealed to Moses
   c. The pillar of fire revealed to the Israelites
   d. The stranger who wrestled Jacob

3. What were the three tests used to distinguish a true prophet from a false prophet?
   a. Call, miracles, and fulfillment of prophecy
   b. Call, visions, and verbal ministry
   c. Call, diet, and the Nazarite vow
   d. Call, mission, and fulfillment of prophecy

4. Who or what is the supreme revelation of God?
   a. Scripture
   b. Creation
   c. Conscience
   d. Christ

5. In the New Testament, what is the chief counterpart to the Old Testament prophet?
   a. Elder
   b. Deacon
   c. Prophetess
   d. Apostle

6. Since Paul was not an eyewitness of the resurrection, he lacks the credentials of being an Apostle.
   a. True
   b. False

DISCUSSION QUESTIONS

1. What is the difference between mediate and immediate general revelation?

2. Explain how special revelation is different from general, and discuss the different modes of special revelation.

3. Read Hebrews 1. What impact does this teaching have on our discussion of God's revelation to man?

5

Inspiration and Authority of Scripture

INTRODUCTION

The Reformation slogan *sola Scriptura*, meaning "Scripture alone," has its origins in Martin Luther's conflict at the Diet of Worms. The Reformers firmly believed that the Bible is the very Word of God. In this lesson, Dr. Sproul highlights how the Reformers' stance on the inspiration and authority of Scripture is relevant for the study of theology today.

MESSAGE OVERVIEW

I. The material cause of the Reformation was the doctrine of justification by faith alone. But lurking behind the scenes was the question of authority.
   a. The slogan *sola Scriptura* means that Scripture alone has the absolute right to bind our consciences.
   b. Counsels and creeds do not have this same authority.
      i. The authority and authorship of the Bible
      ii. "Thus saith the Lord" shows the tension between the divine and human authors of Scripture.
      iii. *Verbum Dei* and *Vox Dei*

II. This leads us to the nature of inspiration.
   a. Second Timothy 3:16 is the primary text that teaches this doctrine.
   b. The English translation of 2 Timothy 3:16 and the way we use the term inspiration in theological language must be distinguished. The key word is "theopneustos." All of Scripture is breathed out by God—expiration.
   c. How does God superintend the writing of Scripture by human authors?
      i. We don't know exactly how this happens from Scripture, but we know what it is not—mechanical inspiration.
      ii. The Council of Trent and "dictate"

iii. The human writers' personalities came through, but were carefully guarded by God from inflicting sin upon the texts.
iv. Verbal inspiration and "jot and tittle" inspiration
v. Liberal and neo-orthodox ideas
vi. The Bible as a witness to revelation, but not as revelation itself

STUDY QUESTIONS

1. What is the Reformed position concerning councils, creeds, and confessions?
   a. They are on the same level of authority as Scripture.
   b. They are secondary to the supreme authority of Scripture.
   c. They are not necessary for the Christian to belief.
   d. They are the supreme authority for faith and practice.

2. What is the process whereby God breathed out His Word?
   a. Inspiration
   b. Interpretation
   c. Inerrancy
   d. Illumination

3. What is the view of inspiration that claims God overrode the personalities of the human authors in the writing of Scripture?
   a. Impersonal
   b. Mechanical
   c. Unconscious
   d. Mysterious

4. What is the precise manner in which God inspired the biblical writers to record His Word?
   a. God dictated His words to them.
   b. God impressed upon their subconscious what He wanted to be written.
   c. God gave them historical events to analyze.
   d. We do not know.

5. Historically, the church has believed that the inspiration of the Bible is verbal, extending to very words of Scripture.
   a. True
   b. False

6. In addition to the words of the Bible, what else did Jesus argue was inspired in Scripture?
   a. Jot and tittle
   b. Complete phrases
   c. Entire paragraphs
   d. The books of Moses

DISCUSSION QUESTIONS

1. What were the two main causes of the Reformation?

2. What is the relationship between authority and authorship of the Bible?

3. How much do we know about the way God inspired Scripture? What are some examples of wrong ideas about it?

4. What is propositional revelation?

6

Infallibility and Inerrancy

INTRODUCTION

Scripture's infallibility and inerrancy have come under attack, particularly through the rise of higher criticism in recent centuries. In this lesson, Dr. Sproul defines infallibility and inerrancy and explains why they are critically important for the Bible to serve as the authoritative rule for faith and life.

MESSAGE OVERVIEW

I. Discussions of the nature of Scripture must deal with matters of infallibility and inerrancy. Both have come under attack in recent years.

II. Inerrancy is alleged to be a creation of the Protestant Scholastics of the seventeenth century, foreign to the biblical writers and the Reformers.
   a. Luther said the Scriptures never err. That seems clear.
   b. Arguments for inerrancy can be very simplistic and faulty. That does not mean inerrancy is false, though.

III. Infallibility is a higher claim than inerrancy. One can be inerrant as a human for a short period of time or in a very specific sense. But infallible means that a document or person never errs in any way.
   a. Conservatives say that the Bible is the only infallible rule of faith and practice.
   b. Others use a similar phrase with a much different meaning. They say, "Only infallible when it speaks to matters of faith and practice."
      i. The first uses the word "only" to point to the uniqueness of the Bible.
      ii. The second uses the word "only" to restrict infallibility to certain sections of Scripture. This is "limited" infallibility.

IV. The question of the authority of the Bible rests upon the authority of Christ.
   a. *God's Inerrant Word* was published in the early 1970s from a conference on inerrancy.
   b. Each scholar had a view of the Bible that was fueled by their view of Christ. Their question was, "What did Jesus think about the Bible?" Even liberal scholars agree that Jesus had an exalted view of Scripture.
   c. Jesus was limited in His knowledge, as touching His human nature. But could He have been wrong? Not and remain sinless. If He taught error, He was subject to judgment, having lied about God and His Word.

V. If the Bible is a basically reliable historical document, then accept it on that level. Then note the basic teachings about Christ, the claims He makes about Himself, and the claims He makes about Scripture. If these claims are basically reliable, then accept His declaration and look for discrepancies to disprove His claims. If you find them, then you have disproved the Bible. If you don't, then you must accept them.

STUDY QUESTIONS

1. What word is used either to highlight the Bible's unique infallibility, or to limit that infallibility?
   a. Completely
   b. Exclusively
   c. Merely
   d. Only

2. It is possible for Scripture to be infallible without also being inerrant.
   a. True
   b. False

3. If you believe that Jesus could have been wrong, what are you challenging about His person?
   a. His humanity
   b. His wisdom
   c. His compassion
   d. His sinlessness

4. What did Dr. Sproul say that we do *not* have assurance of if we reject the Bible as inerrant concerning miracles, morality, science, or history?
   a. God
   b. Christ
   c. Paul
   d. Satan

5. Why do we believe the Bible is the only infallible rule for faith and practice?
   a. It does not contain errors.
   b. The Bible claims to be the word of God.
   c. It is the rule that is delegated by Jesus Christ Himself.
   d. It speaks infallibly only when it speaks of faith and practice.

6. *Inerrancy* is alleged to be the creation of what theological movement?
   a. 16th century Reformation
   b. 17th century scholasticism
   c. 18th century Enlightenment
   d. 19th century liberalism

DISCUSSION QUESTIONS

1. What are the definitions of infallibility and inerrancy?

2. What was Christ's view of the Bible?

3. What are some objections people have to the perfections of the Bible?

4. Some believe they have found errors in the Bible. How do you explain apparent errors in the Bible? What are some helpful resources that focus on these difficult sections of Scripture?

7

Canonicity

INTRODUCTION

The question of canon asks, How do we know the right books have been included in the Bible? In this lesson, Dr. Sproul explores this question and discusses the scope of the Scriptures and how far the canon of Scripture extends.

MESSAGE OVERVIEW

I. What is the Holy Bible?
   a. *Biblios* is the Greek word for Bible.
   b. How do we know that the right 66 books have been included? This is the question of canonicity.
   c. Canon is from the Greek word *kanon*, which means "measuring rod."
   d. Scripture is the *norma normans et sine normativa:* it is the standard and has no peer.

II. What is the scope of the canon?
   a. Of the thousands of possible books, says the critic, only 66 were chosen. Isn't it likely that mistakes were made? Not really. The overwhelming majority of the other candidates were obvious frauds.
   b. Only three books were given serious consideration for inclusion but did not make the canon: The Didache, the Shepherd of Hermas, and the Epistle of Clement. Hebrews, James, 2 Peter, John's epistles, and Jude were not accepted by all immediately.
   c. Another misconception is that it took 500 years to decide on the canon. It was 398 A.D. when the process of canonization was completed. But from the beginning of the church, the New Testament books were used and had functional canonicity.
   d. The heretic Marcion created the first canon. He eliminated books that he did not like and kept those that fit his theology. This action, not any confusion in the church, made it necessary for the church to make the canon official.

III. What was the three-fold test for the canonicity of books?

a. Apostolic origin was important. To meet this criteria, a book had to be written by an apostle or by the direct sanction of an apostle.

- What about Luke and Mark, neither of whom were apostles? The authority of Paul stood behind Luke, and that of Peter stood behind Mark. There was no debate about these gospels because of the oversight of the apostles.

b. The second test was that the book must have been received gladly by the early church.

c. The third test was whether the book in question was in agreement with the books already in the canon. The "core" books of the canon, the ones which were accepted without argument, stood in judgment of other books. For instance, Hebrews 6 was questioned as being out of sorts with apostolic teaching. This was resolved, however, when the early church concluded that Hebrews was written by Paul.

IV. Is the canon infallible?

a. Did the Jewish canon include the Apocrypha?

b. Did the Alexandrian canon (Greek-speaking Jews) have the Apocrypha?

c. The Protestant view of the canon says that each book in the Bible is infallible. But the historic process that the church took was fallible. It appeared to be guided by the Holy Spirit, but the church was not (and is not) infallible in its pronouncements. So we have a fallible collection of infallible books.

d. The Roman Catholic view is that we have an infallible collection of infallible books. The church could not (and does not) err in her official pronouncements.

e. The church did the right thing. We have no reason not to be fully assured that we have a perfect canon.

STUDY QUESTIONS

1. What question does canonicity seek to answer in relation to the biblical writings?
   a. Which books should be included?
   b. Which authors wrote the books?
   c. What genres are the books?
   d. What doctrines are taught in Scripture?

2. Who considers the books of the Apocrypha as canonical, whereas historic Protestantism does not?
   a. Judaism
   b. The Roman Catholic Church
   c. The Eastern Orthodox Church
   d. The church fathers

3. What existed before the formal process of canonization was finished?
   a. A false canon
   b. A universal canon
   c. A functional canon
   d. A politicized canon

4. The Protestant view of the canon is that we have an infallible collection of infallible books.
   a. True
   b. False

5. What heretic, in producing his own canon, forced the church to give an authoritative list of the biblical books?
   a. Arius
   b. Marcion
   c. Pelagius
   d. Ebion

6. What was the threefold test used to determine canonical authenticity?
   a. Apostolic origin, church reception, and doctrinal continuity
   b. Apostolic origin, church reception, and patristic verification
   c. Apostolic origin, government endorsement, and doctrinal continuity
   d. Patristic origin, church reception, and doctrinal continuity

DISCUSSION QUESTIONS

1. What is the definition of the word *canon*?

2. What grounds do we have for confidence in our present canon?

3. What were the criteria of canonicity used by the early church?

4. What is the difference between the Protestant canon and the Roman Catholic canon? How did this difference arise?

5. Is the canon of Scripture infallible? Explain.

8

Scripture and Authority

INTRODUCTION

God does not give us Scripture to be an abstract doctrine but to be His divine Word that fully equips us to be men and women of God. In this lesson, Dr. Sproul walks through Scripture's nature, origin, and authority, and considers how the Bible's authority relates to the church.

MESSAGE OVERVIEW

I. Dr. Sproul's story of Charlie and the inspiration of Scripture.

II. What is the relationship between Scripture and tradition?
  a. The Council of Trent, fourth session, spoke directly to this question. It stated that the revelation of God comes through Scripture and holy tradition. This is called the "dual source" of revelation.
  b. The fourth session of Trent was dismissed abruptly because of war. We know now that the first draft of the session contained the words *partim partim*. That is, the revelation of God is found partially in Scripture and partially in tradition. This wording was protested by two priests, but we don't know how the assembly responded to them. But in the place of *partim partim* in the final draft was simply the word *et*, or "and." Did they repudiate the dual source theory? History says no.
  c. The Catholic response to the "I'll only believe it if it's in the Bible" argument is to say that the Bible gets its authority from the church. It was by the church's decision that certain books were canonized. But this in no way makes the Bible subject to the church.
  d. Catholics go on to teach apostolic succession, further undergirding their view of the pope as the vicar of the church, with Christ as his head.

e. The church used a term to describe the generation of the canon: *recipio*. The church did not arrogantly claim to have created the canon; it said it "received" the canon. This humble reception of the Scriptures reveals a subordination to them, not authority over them.

III. We have spoken in abstract terms about the nature of God's revelation to us. But if we have no mastery of the content of His revelation, we are still ignorant of God's will for us in faith or practice.

- While this series is important, *Dust to Glory* can help you learn fundamental principles for interpreting the Bible. *Knowing Scripture* is also helpful for understanding hermeneutics.

STUDY QUESTIONS

1. What view states that revelation refers to Scripture and tradition?
   a. Rule of faith
   b. *Sola Scriptura*
   c. Dual-source theory
   d. Principle of bivalence

2. In changing the words *partim-partim* to *et*, the Council of Trent repudiated the "dual-source" doctrine.
   a. True
   b. False

3. What was the early church's belief concerning the biblical canon?
   a. They received it.
   b. They discovered it.
   c. They authorized it.
   d. They invented it.

4. What effect should the authority of the Bible have on those who study it, according to the lecture?
   a. It should humble them.
   b. It should boost their self-esteem.
   c. It should cause them to evangelize.
   d. It should elicit worship from them.

5. What is the church's relationship to the Scriptures?
   a. The church shares authority with Scripture.
   b. The church is subordinate to Scripture.
   c. The church created the Scripture.
   d. The church was created by Scripture.

6. What discipline deals with the background issues surrounding systematic theology?
   a. Biblical theology
   b. Prolegomena
   c. Exegesis
   d. Historical theology

DISCUSSION QUESTIONS

1. What is the relationship between Scripture and tradition in the Protestant church?

2. What is the relationship between Scripture and tradition in the Catholic church?

3. What other sources or institutions vie for the authority that belongs to Scripture alone?

9

Knowledge of God

INTRODUCTION

Even though our knowledge of God is neither exhaustive nor comprehensive, we can still speak about Him in a way that is meaningful and true. In this lesson, Dr. Sproul reminds us that God has spoken to us in terms that we can understand and that He has made us in His image, which enables meaningful communication between God and us.

MESSAGE OVERVIEW

I. Soon after it began, Ligonier Ministries hired a consultant to help it define its purpose by asking specific questions. Dr. Sproul's answer to one of his questions was that Ligonier existed to help people find out who God is. As people understand the character of God, so they will understand every other doctrine of God.

II. What is the first thing you study in theology proper?
   a. The *incomprehensibility of God* is the first area of study. Is this some kind of grand disclaimer? No; *incomprehensible* in this context means that our knowledge of God is always partial. Even in heaven, we will not exhaustively comprehend God.
      i. *Finitum non capax infiniti*: The infinite cannot be contained
      ii. God lisps for our benefit.
      iii. Anthropomorphic language is applied to normal descriptions and academic ones.
   b. In what ways can we speak about God?
      i. *Via negativa:* He is not like us and His creation.
      ii. *Via eminentiae:* He is like us, only exalted.

III. We use three kinds of language to describe God.

a. The term *univocal* means "having only one meaning." In theology, it describes characteristics that we share with God.

b. *Equivocal* means "having two meanings." It describes a term that radically changes its definition depending upon the one to whom it is referring.

c. *Analogical* means "likeness or similarity." Analogical language is a representation based on proportion. The meaning changes in direct relationship to that which is described, i.e., the good dog, good God, good man.

STUDY QUESTIONS

1. What does the doctrine of incomprehensibility of God really mean?
   a. Our knowledge of God is exhaustive.
   b. Knowledge of God is impossible.
   c. Knowledge of God is self-contradictory.
   d. Our knowledge of God is partial and limited.

2. What is the meaning behind the phrase *Finitum non capax infiniti?*
   a. The finite cannot know the infinite.
   b. The infinite cannot be contained.
   c. The finite must become infinite.
   d. The infinite cannot grasp the finite.

3. Because we deny any sort of double standard, we must always affirm God's characteristics in their univocal sense.
   a. True
   b. False

4. In what way are we speaking when we acknowledge that God is like us, but infinitely above us?
   a. Equivocally
   b. Transcendentally
   c. Analogically
   d. Univocally

5. What Reformer likened God's interactions with His creatures to a lisp?
   a. Martin Luther
   b. Ulrich Zwingli
   c. Erasmus of Rotterdam
   d. John Calvin

6. What is one of the most common ways in theology that we speak about or describe God?
    a. *Via negationis*
    b. *Via cognitionis*
    c. *Via eminentiae*
    d. *Via affirmatos*

DISCUSSION QUESTIONS

1. What do we normally mean by the word *incomprehensible*? What does it mean in theology?

2. When we say that God lisps when He talks to us, what do we mean?

3. When we speak of God, we generally use two broad methods: saying what He is and what He is not. What are some examples of this language in the Bible?

4. The last three terms Dr. Sproul used are universal, applying to our descriptions of any idea or object. Using an example of your own creation, make univocal, equivocal, and analogical descriptions of it.

10

One in Essence

INTRODUCTION

The oneness of God is so central to the religious life of His people that the book of Deuteronomy commands it to be taught to their children on a daily basis. In this lesson, Dr. Sproul discusses the truth that our God is on in essence.

MESSAGE OVERVIEW

I. Pagans of all types lack an understanding of the unity of God. In the midst of many polytheistic cultures, Judaism fiercely clung to monotheism.
   a. Some say the Jews were not monotheists, but that redactors have edited the Bible to make it appear so. But those critical theories do not handle the multiple evidences from multiple sources testifying of the religion of the Jews.
   b. The Jews put great stress on the singularity of God. The *Shema,* found in Deuteronomy 6:4, is at the core of Jewish spirituality.
   c. The Jews did not take the prescription in the *Shema* as hyperbole. They were so serious about their monotheism, they literally placed the message of it on their foreheads, doorposts, and arms. They regularly taught their children the command that they should "have no other God before Me."

II. The Trinity is a difficult, mysterious doctrine, yet it is taught in Scripture.
   a. How can Christians be faithful to the religion of the Old Testament and hold an orthodox doctrine of the Trinity?
   b. This question is not answered by a simple investigation of the history of theology. The New Testament is the key to unlocking much of the confusion surrounding the Trinity.
   c. John 1:1 is a key text for understanding God's unity and plurality.
   d. The Greek word *logos* is translated as "word." In the beginning, the *Logos* was with the Father. One person was with another person.

e. "With" is also a key word in this text. There are three ways this English word is brought through from the Greek. In this case, the Greek word translated as "with" in this passage is *pros,* which means "face to face intimacy." Jesus was intimately associated with the Father.

f. The verse also says that Jesus not only was with God, but that He was God. The Word is differentiated from God, but is also identified with God. It was because of plain teaching like this in the New Testament that the church developed the doctrine of the Trinity.

III. There are other references to the Trinity in the New Testament.

a. The testimony of Thomas, who cried out "My Lord and my God!" as he witnessed his resurrected Lord, plainly shows that Jesus is God.

b. Jesus stated several times that He was God, for instance when He said He was Lord of the sabbath or when He said He was given all authority. Also, for Jesus to say that He was the way, the truth, and the life was a clear testimony from Jesus' lips that He believed He was God.

c. The distinctions of each person of the Godhead do not destroy Their deity. Neither does emphasizing the deity of each person do away with Their distinctions.

STUDY QUESTIONS

1. The Jews were polytheists until later scholars edited the Old Testament to teach monotheism.
   a. True
   b. False

2. Which of the following terms is an accurate way to describe the Trinity?
   a. Contradictory
   b. Mysterious
   c. Unknowable
   d. Erroneous

3. What does the prologue to the gospel of John teach about Jesus' relationship to God?
   a. He was with God and was known by God.
   b. He was with God and was created by God.
   c. He was with God and was the same person as the Father.
   d. He was with God and He was God.

4. What is the historic formulation of the Trinity?
   a. God is one person who expresses Himself in three ways.
   b. God is one in person and three in essence.
   c. God is one in essence and three in person.
   d. God is one God among three.

5. What Greek word is related to John's description of the closeness the Son shared between the Father?
   a. *Logos*
   b. *Sun*
   c. *Meta*
   d. *Prosōpon*

6. In the first 300 years of the church's reflection, what description for Jesus dominated the thinking of early church theologians?
   a. Door of the sheep
   b. Lamb of God
   c. Lion of Judah
   d. The *Logos*

DISCUSSION QUESTIONS

1. What does the term "polytheism" mean? What does "monotheism" mean?

2. How does the *Shema* illustrate the importance of monotheism to the Jews?

3. How does John 1 teach a doctrine of the Trinity? What other New Testament passages teach this doctrine, affirming the unity of God yet also affirming the distinctions in His persons?

4. Can someone be a Christian without believing in the Trinity? Why or why not?

11

Three in Person

INTRODUCTION

Many argue the doctrine of the Trinity is a contradiction and that Christians worship three gods instead of one. In this lesson, Dr. Sproul demonstrates that, while the doctrine of the Trinity is mysterious, it is by no means contradictory.

MESSAGE OVERVIEW

I. Is the Trinity a contradiction?
   a. Many people say yes, but it is surprising that some educated people say so based on logic. The formula for the Trinity is paradoxical, but not contradictory.
   b. "One in essence, three in person" is the classical statement of the Trinity. This formula does not violate the law of non-contradiction, because it is not referring to the same thing at the same time and in the same relationship. God is not both one and three at the same time and in the same relationship.

II. What is a paradox?
   a. The word *paradox* is made up of two Greek roots: *para* (alongside) and *dox* (seem, appear).
   b. A paradox occurs when two things, placed alongside each other, appear to be contradictory. But when you look closely, you can see that there is no contradiction.
      i. Essence: being, substance, stuff
      ii. Person: "masks" that actors wore to appear as different characters

III. What is subsistence?
   • It is not someone who is basically surviving on meager food; in theology, it means a person who functions under another one.

   i. God cannot exist in the technical sense of the word.
   ii. The Father, Son, and Holy Spirit subsist, not exist.
   iii. One being, three persons

STUDY QUESTIONS

1. Which logical term can be applied to the doctrine of the Trinity?
   a. Contradiction
   b. Paradox
   c. Fallacy
   d. Syllogism

2. What word acts as a synonym for the informal word *stuff*?
   a. Essence
   b. Person
   c. Existence
   d. Paradox

3. How was the Latin word *persona* originally used?
   a. As a legal and philosophical term
   b. As a theatrical and theological term
   c. As a philosophical and theatrical term
   d. As a legal and theatrical term

4. It is accurate to speak of God existing.
   a. True
   b. False

5. What is another way to describe the persons of the Trinity?
   a. As subsistences
   b. As substances
   c. As existences
   d. As beings

6. We say that the distinctions among the three persons are necessary, but what are the distinctions *not*?
   a. They are not real.
   b. They are not applicable.
   c. They are not biblical.
   d. They are not essential.

DISCUSSION QUESTIONS

1. What is the law of non-contradiction? Does the Trinity break it? What if it did?

2. What is a paradox? How is the Trinity a paradox? Are there any other doctrines that appear to be contradictions at first glance?

3. In the definition of the Trinity, essence and person are important words. Explain what Dr. Sproul said they mean in this context.

4. What does subsistence mean in a theological context? Why is it a superior description of God compared to existence?

12

Incommunicable Attributes

INTRODUCTION

When we study the doctrine of God, one of the most important things we're concerned with is an understanding of His attributes. In this lesson, Dr. Sproul distinguishes between the communicable and the incommunicable attributes of God and the practical ramifications they have for our lives.

MESSAGE OVERVIEW

I. A form of identification usually is required for purchases on credit. When we identify someone we are looking for traits, and combined, these traits are the person's attributes. God is identified by His attributes, but they are broken into two groups.
    a. Communicable attributes are those which also are found in humans, but to a lesser degree.
    b. Incommunicable attributes are those which are found in God alone.

II. What are the incommunicable attributes?
    a. Is it possible for God to create another "god"?
        i. No, because the new god would not be independent, uncreated; there are certain attributes that God cannot transfer from Himself.
        ii. Simplicity of God
    b. What are some of the differences between God and man?
        i. We are human beings, but God is supreme. The real difference between God and man is that His being is very different from ours. He is independent, but we are entirely dependent on Him. What He creates, He sustains.
        ii. Who caused God? John Stuart Mill erred in his understanding of the law of causality. Can He be self-creating? No. But He is self-existent.
        iii. Aseity: self-existence of God
    c. The one who is supreme deserves our worship and our awe.

STUDY QUESTIONS

1. The notion of something being self-existent is what?
   a. A scientific absurdity
   b. An illogical contradiction
   c. A rational possibility
   d. An irrational possibility

2. God cannot transfer His incommunicable attributes to us, but He could transfer them to create another god.
   a. True
   b. False

3. What are theologians saying when they speak of God as transcendent?
   a. God is a higher order of being than other beings.
   b. God is beyond comprehension.
   c. God is beautiful.
   d. God is absent from His creation.

4. What law did John Stuart Mill misunderstand when he argued against the existence God?
   a. The law of non-contradiction
   b. The law of identity
   c. The law of reflexivity
   d. The law of causality

5. What do we mean when we say that God is simple?
   a. God is easy to understand.
   b. God is simplistic.
   c. God does not possess all knowledge.
   d. God is not made up of parts.

6. What do we call God when we distinguish Him from His creatures?
   a. The Lord of Hosts
   b. The Sustainer of Life
   c. The Redeemer
   d. The Supreme Being

DISCUSSION QUESTIONS

1. What are some examples of communicable attributes? Incommunicable?

2. In what sense is God "simple"?

3. In what areas are God and man fundamentally different?

4. What does “aseity” mean and why is it such an important theological idea?

13

Communicable Attributes

INTRODUCTION

God's communicable attributes are those characteristics that He shares with His creation. In this lesson, Dr. Sproul explores the attributes of God and explains their importance for godly living.

MESSAGE OVERVIEW

I. There are communicable and incommunicable attributes.
   a. Ephesians 5:1: "Therefore be *imitators* of God as dear children."
   b. We can imitate God only if there are certain things we share with Him, certain attributes that are communicable.
   c. One attribute is debatable: holiness.
   d. Why is the word *holy* attached to the third person of the Trinity?
   e. Does redemption include deification, as stated by the Eastern Orthodox?

II. What are the communicable attributes?
   a. Paul confirms that love is shared by God and humans.
   b. The goodness of God can be imitated.
   c. God is just, and we are called to be workers of justice as well. Both internally and externally, God is just.
   d. We are not sinners because we sin; we sin because we are sinners.
   e. God is wise, and we are instructed by books such as Proverbs, James, and Song of Solomon to be wise also.

STUDY QUESTIONS

1. Regeneration not only enables us to share in the communicable attributes of God, but also involves the deification of humanity.
   a. True
   b. False

2. Which attribute should not be confused with God's justice?
   a. Patience
   b. Love
   c. Injustice
   d. Mercy

3. Which attribute is both a communicable and incommunicable attribute of God?
   a. Love
   b. Justice
   c. Wisdom
   d. Holiness

4. What did God give us that we might be wise?
   a. His Spirit
   b. His Holiness
   c. His Word
   d. His Love

5. What other discipline does the Old Testament distinguish wisdom from?
   a. Obedience
   b. Knowledge
   c. Service
   d. Oration

6. Who did Jesus say was the only one who is good?
   a. God
   b. Man
   c. John
   d. Jesus

DISCUSSION QUESTIONS

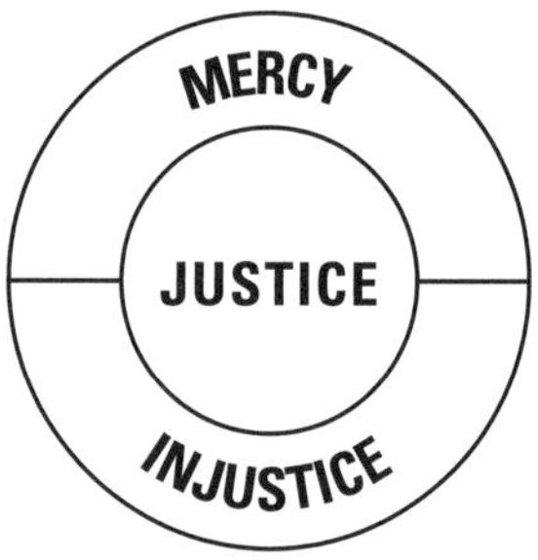

1. What is the main difference between communicable and incommunicable attributes?

2. Why is it debatable as to whether holiness is shared by humans?

3. Name five communicable attributes. How do humans obtain these attributes?

4. Notice the diagram. How does this help us understand how it is righteous for God to have mercy on some but not others?

14

The Will of God

INTRODUCTION

Many obedient Christians earnestly wonder what God's will is for their lives. However, when we discuss the will of God, we need to make a distinction between God's revealed will and God's hidden will. In this lesson, Dr. Sproul explores these distinctions and explains how to apply them according to His Word.

MESSAGE OVERVIEW

I. The Primary "Ask R.C." Question: How can I know the will of God for my life?
   a. Deut. 29:29: "The secret things belong to the Lord. . . ."
   b. Where is this quotation found? It is in the second book of the Law, during recapitulation of the Law given through Moses.

II. Hidden and Revealed Will of God
   a. *Deus absconditus:* (Latin) The Hidden God.
   b. *Deus revelatus:* (Latin) The Revealed God.
   c. These two concepts are found in Deuteronomy 29:29.

III. Uses of the Term "Will of God"
   a. The Decretive Will: What God sovereignly, absolutely, efficaciously, brings to pass. It is what He has determined will occur.
   b. The Preceptive Will: What God has spoken as right and true. It can be and quite frequently is resisted.
   c. "How can I know God's will?" is a question that demands a follow-up: "What kind of will are you talking about?"
   d. "Where God closes His holy mouth, I will desist from inquiry" (John Calvin) or, "The hidden will of God is none of your business."

   e. This explains the practical reasons behind God's restrictions concerning divination.

IV. What do the Scriptures say?.
   a. "This is the will of God for you, even your sanctification" 1 Thess. 4:3.
   b. How do you know which job? Which mate? Study the preceptive will of God and learn how to live day to day. Study God's law, and find a way to live that most fulfills His holy commands.
   c. Tomorrow is the surest revelation of the hidden will of God.
   d. "But the things revealed belong to us. . . ." Note to whom the revealed things belong. They belong to our children and us.
   e. Even though we have the New Testament revelation of Christ, we may still use the law as it reveals the character of God.

STUDY QUESTIONS

1. According to Deuteronomy 29:29, we cannot know the will of God.
   a. True
   b. False

2. Which of the following describes the will by which God ordains everything that comes to pass?
   a. God's preceptive will
   b. God's decretive will
   c. God's permissive will
   d. God's decisive will

3. What practice is a sinful attempt to search out the future will of God?
   a. Prediction
   b. Discernment
   c. Speculation
   d. Divination

4. What should we do if we want to know the preceptive will of God?
   a. Study the law.
   b. Study natural revelation.
   c. Study the stars.
   d. Study our hearts.

5. What did Dr. Sproul emphasize in this lecture as God's will for us?
   a. That we trust in Christ
   b. That we abstain from sexual immorality
   c. That we do justice and love mercy
   d. That we obey the Word of God

6. Who said "Where God closes His holy mouth, I will desist from inquiry"?
    a. John Knox
    b. John Calvin
    c. Theodore Beza
    d. Philipp Melanchthon

DISCUSSION QUESTIONS

1. What is the #1 question you have concerning Christianity?

2. How has God revealed Himself in creation and in the Bible? In what way has He hidden Himself?

3. What are the differences between the preceptive will and the decretive will of God?

4. What are some examples of topics in the Bible that God has whispered about rather than shouted about? How should God's relative silence on a particular topic guide us as we take a stand on that topic?

5. Explain how God is not unjust by not electing everyone to salvation.

15

Providence

INTRODUCTION

The secular mind-set says that God is a spectator in heaven with no control over what happens on earth. Yet Christians have always had an acute sense that this is our Father's world and that the affairs of men and nations are in His hands. In this lesson, Dr. Sproul highlights that God is actively involved in preserving His creation, even working His will through our intentional decisions.

MESSAGE OVERVIEW

I. Paul says in Romans 8:28 that God causes all things to work for the good of those who love Him. This is stated with extraordinary strength.
   a. How do our lives relate to the sovereign government of God? Our thoughts on this matter have changed radically since the founding of our country, even since the Civil War.
   b. Romans 8:28–30: "And we know that all things work together for good to those who love God, to those who are the called according to His purpose. For whom He foreknew, He also predestined to be conformed to the image of His Son, that He might be the firstborn among many brethren. Moreover whom He predestined, these He also called; whom He called, these He also justified; and whom He justified, these He also glorified."
   c. "What then shall we say to these things?" What is our response? "If God is for us, who can be against us?" *Deus pro nobis* means "God for us."

II. What is providence?
   a. The root of this word means "to see." The prefix means "beforehand." But this word, theologically, does not simply mean foreknowledge. It is more akin to "provision."
   b. We are first introduced to the idea of providence in Genesis 22.

   c. Providence covers several areas.
      i. Sustaining or preserving
      ii. Provision
   d. What is the doctrine of concurrence?
      i. Is God the author of sin?
      ii. What you meant for evil, God meant for good.
      iii. Judas and concurrence

STUDY QUESTIONS

1. What word refers chiefly to God's government of creation?
   a. Covenant
   b. Providence
   c. Foresight
   d. Concurrence

2. The promise of God in Romans 8:28–30 means that everything will go well in life for Christians.
   a. True
   b. False

3. What word is closest in meaning to the word *providence?*
   a. Fortune
   b. Perseverance
   c. Provision
   d. Preservation

4. What does the phrase *Deus pro nobis* mean?
   a. God with us
   b. God over us
   c. God before us
   d. God for us

5. In which Old Testament story do we first encounter the use of the word *providence*?
   a. Moses and the Burning Bush
   b. Abraham offering up Isaac
   c. Joseph sold into slavery
   d. Isaac and Rebekah

6. What is the Hebrew word for *create*?
   a. *Yada*
   b. *Ruach*
   c. *Bara'*
   d. *Berith*

DISCUSSION QUESTIONS

1. Why is Paul so sure about what he says in Romans 8:28? What other evidence for this is found in Scripture?

2. What does the word *providence* mean?

3. Where is providence first mentioned in the Bible?

4. What are some areas that providence covers?

5. What is the doctrine of concurrence? Read Deuteronomy 29:29—do we ever know for sure exactly how God's will and sin interface?

16

Creatio Ex Nihilo

INTRODUCTION

God created all things *ex nihilo*, "out of nothing." By the command of His word, all things came into being. In this lesson, Dr. Sproul introduces the Christian doctrine of creation and shows how it is different from secular and atheistic views of creation.

MESSAGE OVERVIEW

I. What is the doctrine of creation?
   a. The central issue that separates secularism and supernatural religion is the doctrine of creation.
   b. In the beginning, God created the heavens and the earth.
      i. Beginning
      ii. God
      iii. Creation

II. What was the beginning of the universe like?
   a. Even most secularists acknowledge the universe had a beginning. But the nature of that beginning is disputed.
   b. Some might even debate whether there is a universe at all, i.e., a solipsist.
   c. There are three basic options for answering the questions of creation.
      i. Eternal (self-existent)
      ii. Created by someone who is self-existent (includes Christian worldview)
      iii. Self-created (irrational)
   d. Spontaneous generation is the conceptual grandfather of the self-creation hypothesis.

e. Chance is a legitimate scientific concept to be used when trying to discover mathematical possibilities. But chance is not a being or power. It cannot influence anything. It is a mathematical entity, not a thing.
f. The idea of a self-existent material world is a popular idea. It is thought that there is a stable, self-existent part of the universe somewhere. That portion is like a power core, or battery. So there is no need for a transcendent being to create or sustain the visible universe.
g. *Ex nihilo nihil fit* means "out of nothing, nothing comes."
h. *Creatio ex nihilo* teaches that God called the universe into existence. He did not shape or form it from pre-existing material.
i. God gave the word, the divine fiat, and the universe began.

STUDY QUESTIONS

1. What does *ex nihilo* mean?
   a. "Created out of nothing"
   b. "All things from nothing"
   c. "From nothing"
   d. "Out of nothing"

2. The idea of spontaneous generation is flatly rejected by the scientific community today.
   a. True
   b. False

3. Which theory of origins denies the existence of the universe?
   a. Self-existent
   b. Created
   c. Self-creation
   d. Illusion

4. To what do most scientists attribute the beginning of the universe?
   a. Matter
   b. Intelligent design
   c. Random chance
   d. A transcendent creator

5. What led to the demise of the God hypothesis?
   a. The Enlightenment
   b. The theory of evolution
   c. Spontaneous generation
   d. Chance creation

6. What does Scripture mean when it speaks of God as transcendent?
   a. It means God is in heaven.
   b. It means God is within all things.
   c. It means God is above all things in His being.
   d. It means God is the eternal power of creation.

DISCUSSION QUESTIONS

1. Three terms in Genesis 1:1 define the creation debate. What are they?

2. What is chance?

3. There are three basic options for explaining the nature of the creation of the universe. What are those options?

17

Angels and Demons

INTRODUCTION

Modern man is critical of anything supernatural, but belief in angels and demons is an important part of the Christian faith. In this lesson, Dr. Sproul uses Scripture to explain the role of ministering spirits and the reality of Satan and demons.

MESSAGE OVERVIEW

I. "There can be no biblical theology without demonology," G. C. Berkhower said.
   a. Rudolf Bultmann attacked the veracity of the New Testament by attacking the supernatural worldview of the first century.
   b. The world the New Testament describes is filled with angels and demons. Therefore, that world is deemed to be faulty.
   c. What is it about Satan that is so unbelievable? The current image of Satan was developed during the Middle Ages. The people of the time mocked him and joked about him so as to attack his pride.

II. In the teachings of Christ angels are discussed more than love or sin. Does this validate the current New Age interest in angels? No.
   a. An early heresy in the church was that Jesus was actually an angel. The author of Hebrews challenges that assumption. See Hebrews 1.
   b. Angels are created beings who have various functions.
      i. Mysterious: invisible, visible, various shapes and forms
      ii. Ministering spirits: seraphim, cherubim; help to Jesus
      iii. Messengers: announce John's and Jesus' births, make Old Testament visits
   c. How do fallen angels differ? They are lesser angels who fell with Satan and are under his command. Satan is not God. Particularly, he is not all-knowing and all-present. Do not attribute too much power to Satan.

    i. Tempter
    ii. Deceiver
    iii. Accuser (Rev. 12:10)
  d. A warning: Satan, like other angels, is metamorphic. He can change images as easily as we change our clothes. He can appear as pure as light.

STUDY QUESTIONS

1. Belief in angels and demons is often attacked because people reject which of the following?
   a. Superstition
   b. Naturalism
   c. Spuriousness
   d. Supernaturalism

2. The popular pitchfork image of Satan is largely a product of what?
   a. The testimony of God's Word
   b. Enlightenment skepticism
   c. The Middle Ages
   d. Scientific inquiry

3. The Bible rarely speaks about angels in the New Testament.
   a. True
   b. False

4. The early church was greatly concerned with the nature and function of angels because a heresy arose claiming Christ was which of the following?
   a. An angel
   b. A supernatural being
   c. A demon
   d. A demigod

5. What is the primary role and function of angels?
   a. Guardians
   b. Warriors
   c. Ministering spirits
   d. Messengers

6. Which of the following do Christians incorrectly attribute to Satan?
   a. Demonic power
   b. Divine nature
   c. Deception
   d. Craftiness

DISCUSSION QUESTIONS

1. What is it about Satan that makes him unbelievable?

2. Angels are created beings. What are the popular ideas about angels that are contradicted by Scripture?

3. What are the various functions of good angels? What are the various evil functions of Satan?

4. What other questions do you have about angels and demons? Does Scripture answer those questions clearly? What do we do with our unanswered questions?

18

The Creation of Man

INTRODUCTION

Various theories of evolution and humanism have changed culture's understanding of man's origin and being. In this lesson, Dr. Sproul defines human beings in terms of their dignity as creatures made in the image of God.

MESSAGE OVERVIEW

I. The creation of man is closely connected to the overall doctrine of creation. With the assault on creation, the dignity of man is also assaulted.
   a. One philosopher has said, "We are at best grown-up germs, sitting on one cog on one wheel of a vast cosmic machine that is destined for annihilation."
   b. Jean-Paul Sartre was one of the most pessimistic of philosophers. He showed the effects of ignoring the dignity that flows from the divine creation of man.
   c. Non-Christians have no reason to give man any dignity. They live on borrowed capital from the Christian worldview.

II. Starting in Genesis 1:26, man's creation is described as initiated by God, just like that of the rest of creation. But we are different in our function and form from the rest of creation.
   a. We are made in the image of God, the *imago Dei*. What is the nature of the discussion?
      i. Image and likeness in Catholicism
      ii. Hendiadys
      iii. Medieval theologians vs. Barth: the analogy of being vs. wholly other
   b. What precisely is the *imago Dei?*
      i. Rational and instinctive
      ii. Volitional

iii. Affect
iv. Male and female: analogy of relationship a la Barth
v. Responsibility and ability
vi. Reasoning back from the Second Adam: a unique ability to mirror the character of God

c. Since the Fall, do we still have the image of God? Yes, though it has been marred.

STUDY QUESTIONS

1. Which of the following depends upon the doctrine of creation?
    a. The happiness of man
    b. The dignity of man
    c. The self-esteem of man
    d. The creativity of man

2. The phrase *imago Dei* means "image of God."
    a. True
    b. False

3. Which did Karl Barth reject?
    a. *Analogia relationis*
    b. *Imago Dei*
    c. *Analogia entis*
    d. *Analogia fidei*

4. What relationship does the *analogia relationis* refer to?
    a. Between humans and animals
    b. Between male and female
    c. Between God and human beings
    d. Between man and creation

5. How are human beings like God?
    a. In our rationality, volition, and affection
    b. In our relational, moral, and spiritual nature
    c. In our mind, feelings, and will
    d. In our faith, hope, and love

6. As emphasized in this lecture, what is the unique mission of the human race?
    a. To multiply and take dominion
    b. To baptize and make disciples
    c. To love God and neighbor
    d. To mirror and reflect God

DISCUSSION QUESTIONS

1. In non-Christian worldviews, how does man obtain dignity?
2. How are we similar to and different from the rest of creation?
3. What are some opinions on the image of God in man? What is the true nature of the image of God in man?
4. Since the Fall, do we still bear the image of God? In what way do sub-cognitive people (the mentally handicapped or infants) bear the image of God?

19

The Nature of Sin

INTRODUCTION

The full measure of sin and its effects in the world are often overlooked, but the Christian doctrine of sin sees the vastness of the problem and takes it very seriously. In this lesson, Dr. Sproul describes the impact of the fall in nature, in our relationship with God, and in our relationships with others.

MESSAGE OVERVIEW

I. Something is very wrong with the world in which we live.
   a. God created the universe in its perfect state, but the fall of mankind brought tragedy and curse upon the entire universe.
   b. There are cosmic ramifications of sin. Because humans were in charge of the entire earth, the earth was cursed along with Adam and humanity.

II. What are the effects of sin upon man and the universe?
   - People are alienated or estranged.
      i. Estranged from nature
      ii. Estranged from God
      iii. Estranged from each other
      iv. Estranged from self

III. What is the nature of sin?
   a. Sin can be defined as "missing the mark," as when an archer misses his bull's-eye. It is the standard or norm of God's law that is the target.
   b. Sin is, according to the Westminster Shorter Catechism, "any want of conformity to, or transgression of, the law of God."

IV. What is the origin of sin?
   a. Did God cause sin?
      i. *Privatio*
      ii. *Negatio*
   b. Sin is primarily defined in negative terms, over against the positive norm of God's character or law. But do not think that just because we define sin negatively that it is not actual. It is real. It is something in which we are personally involved.

STUDY QUESTIONS

1. Sin is a problem limited to mankind.
   a. True
   b. False

2. How has sin primarily affected our relationship with God, one another, and self?
   a. There is now rejection.
   b. There is now embarrassment.
   c. There is need for restoration.
   d. There is now estrangement.

3. *Hamartia*, the Greek word for "sin," was originally a term used in which of the following disciplines?
   a. Archery
   b. Astronomy
   c. Military
   d. Theology

4. What is a transgression?
   a. Another word for sin
   b. An active violation of God's law
   c. A lack of conformity to God's law
   d. A deliberate disobedience

5. Which two words are used to describe the nature of evil?
   a. Privation and negation
   b. Deprivation and disobedience
   c. Unrighteous and ungodliness
   d. Want and transgression

6. What is evil dependent upon?
   a. Satan
   b. The fall
   c. Sin
   d. Good

DISCUSSION QUESTIONS

1. How much of the world is harmed by sin? Why?

2. What are the four ways man is affected by sin?

3. What is the nature of sin?

4. Did God cause sin?

20

Original Sin

INTRODUCTION

The extent and scope of the nature of sin leads to the question of original sin. In this lesson, Dr. Sproul discusses the concept and consequence of the first sin and the controversy surrounding this doctrine.

MESSAGE OVERVIEW

I. A popular misunderstanding is that the doctrine of original sin refers to the first sin. But it is a description of the results of that sin, not that sin itself.
   a. We are not sinners because we sin, but we sin because we are sinners.
   b. Original sin describes the fallen condition of the human race.
   c. Jonathan Edwards said, "If the Bible did not tell us that there is a problem with our moral disposition by nature, we would have to affirm it on the basis of rational observation because of the pervasive presence of evil in the world of human beings."
   d. Even pagans acknowledge that "Nobody's perfect." But if perfection is possible, wouldn't you expect more people to attain and maintain it?
   e. Original sin is a judgment of God upon rational creatures.

II. The classic study of this doctrine was done by St. Augustine and was the center of the Pelagian controversy of the fourth century.
   a. God made man *posse peccare,* or able to sin. Humans had the power to sin. We know that because they sinned.
   b. They also were created *posse non peccare,* or able to not sin. They had the moral ability to obey God.
   c. In the Fall, mankind lost *posse non peccare* and received *non posse, non peccare*. They lost the ability to not sin and received the inability to not sin. This does not mean man cannot do anything to obey the commandments in an outward manner. But he cannot keep them rightly.

III. As an aside, even Christians are subject to this rule. All people are unable to obey God rightly and completely. Amoral things that we refer to as "mistakes" are often rooted in moral matters. If we loved God with our minds, we would not make nearly as many "errors."
   a. Jesus says in John 6:44 that people cannot do the good work of coming to God without the enabling of God. The doctrine of original sin makes the effectual calling of God absolutely necessary.
   b. Many do not agree, and claim that there is an "island of righteousness" in every man. This view is not biblical (Rom. 3:10–11).
   c. We were made in the image of God. We lost the image of God in the narrow sense in the Fall, but we retain it in the broad sense. The perfections granted to us were lost, but the many other similarities God granted us remain.

STUDY QUESTIONS

1. Where do we learn of original sin?
   a. Scripture
   b. Everywhere
   c. Creation
   d. Ourselves

2. Original sin refers to that first sin committed by Adam and Eve.
   a. True
   b. False

3. What does *non posse non peccare* mean?
   a. Both sinner and just
   b. Able to sin
   c. Able not to sin
   d. Not able not to sin

4. What is the inability not to sin called in theology?
   a. Moral inability
   b. Sinless inability
   c. Inability to obey
   d. Perfection inability

5. What is civil virtue?
   a. Obeying the law for praise
   b. Obeying the law on accident
   c. Obeying the law externally
   d. Obeying the law as civic duty

6. Which of the following doctrines is absolutely necessary because of original sin?
   a. Effectual calling
   b. The freedom of the will
   c. Definite atonement
   d. Presumptive regeneration

DISCUSSION QUESTIONS

1. Are we sinners because we sin, or do we sin because we are sinners? Explain.

2. What does original sin describe?

3. What early controversy brought the issue of original sin to center stage?

4. How did Augustine describe the state of man before and after the Fall?

5. What does John 6:44 teach about man's ability to come to God?

21

Transmission of Sin

INTRODUCTION

The connection between Adam's sin and the sins of humanity is explained in the doctrine of the transmission of a sin nature. In this lesson, Dr. Sproul compares the transmission of Adam's sin and the transfer of Christ's righteousness as the second Adam.

MESSAGE OVERVIEW

I. The doctrine of original sin raises the question, "How can God hold us accountable for sin when we cannot do anything but sin?"
   a. How is the sin nature (and therefore guilt) transferred from Adam to us?
   b. Romans 5:12: "Therefore, just as through one man sin entered the world, and death through sin, and thus death spread to all men, because all sinned."
   c. Do we duplicate in our own life the fall of Adam, and therefore make the transfer of guilt unnecessary? No.
   d. How do we know differently? Infants die. They are not active sinners, and the Scriptures tell us why they bear the curse in Romans 5.

II. There are three positions on exactly how Adam's guilt is transferred.
   a. Realism, crass version—It would be just for God to visit us with fallen natures only if we actually sinned. So we were really there in the garden with Adam. Our souls were pre-existent, present in the garden, participating in some way in the Fall. The ministry of Melchizedek is mentioned as "proof" of this, as recorded in Hebrews 7:10.
   b. Realism, sophisticated version—In the mind of God, you pre-existed. He had a perfect idea of you, and this idea was real. If you were there in God's mind, you were really there. But this depends on a platonic view of ideas. Jonathan Edwards held this view.

c. Federalism—Adam represents us, just as Jesus represents us. Adam does not act alone, but acts on our behalf. His probation is our probation since he is our representative.
   i. "No damnation without representation!"
   ii. We were accurately represented and flawlessly represented. God perfectly chose our representative.
   iii. God selects our representative, just as God selected Jesus to represent His elect.

STUDY QUESTIONS

1. What is the idea of the fall in reference to?
   a. To our personal temptation
   b. To the historical fall of Adam
   c. To our individual fall into sin
   d. To a parable for good and evil

2. Who is born without sin?
   a. Infants
   b. Adam's descendants
   c. Jesus Christ
   d. No one

3. Which view of transmission believes our pre-existent souls participated in the fall?
   a. Crass realism
   b. Sophisticated realism
   c. Federalism
   d. Individualism

4. Which system of thought does sophisticated realism depend upon?
   a. Aristotelianism
   b. Gnosticism
   c. Platonism
   d. Alexandrianism

5. How are the sins of Adam transmitted in the federalist view?
   a. Through representation
   b. Through mediation
   c. Through genetics
   d. Through substitution

6. Jesus Christ is the second Adam.
   a. True
   b. False

DISCUSSION QUESTIONS

1. How is God just in passing the consequences of Adam's sin to us?
2. What are some situations that demonstrate the effects of Adam's sin?
3. What are the two kinds of realism?
4. Describe the federal view of the transmission of original sin. How did Adam perfectly represent us?

22

The Covenants

INTRODUCTION

In Scripture, God relates to His people according to covenant. In this lesson, Dr. Sproul outlines the three major covenants that serve as the framework of Scripture.

MESSAGE OVERVIEW

I. In Hebrews 8:3–6, the author says Jesus was mediator of a better covenant that was established on better promises.
   a. The author goes on to explain exactly why the new covenant is a better covenant.
   b. This passage reveals the nature of covenants, demonstrating that the structure of covenant provides a framework for all God's relationships with man.

II. The covenants God has made with man progressed from the covenant made with Adam to one with Noah, then Abraham, then Moses, then David, and then with all believers through Christ.
   a. Covenants are based on the promises of God toward man. They include stipulations—conditions to be fulfilled. Ceremonies follow that dramatize the words of the agreement.
   b. God has given us His word, in Christ, that He will fulfill all He has said.
   c. Jesus' life and ministry were part of the dramatic revelation of the vast expanse of God's promises toward us.

III. There are three major covenants in Scripture.
   a. The covenants of redemption, works, and grace are the three main covenants God has made.
   b. The first is the covenantal agreement that was made in eternity between the persons of the Godhead. As a result, the creation of the world came to be.

And in redemption, the Trinity worked together to bring about the plan of salvation. The Father makes the plan, the Son carries it out, and the Spirit seals our salvation.

c. The second is the covenant God made with Adam. In the probationary scenario of the garden, Adam and Eve covenanted with God to obey him and live. The destiny of the human race was to be decided on the basis of the work of Adam and Eve. They disobeyed, failed the probation, and condemned the world.
d. The covenant of grace promotes us to the state that Adam and Eve would have achieved if they had obeyed God.
e. There was grace in the covenant of works; it was not empty of God's blessing.
f. Confusion sometimes occurs when we read that we are saved by grace (Eph. 2:8–10). Jesus is the new Adam, the one who comes into the world and places Himself under the obligations of the covenant of works. He succeeds where Adam failed. The life and works of Christ save us, so in this sense we are saved by works. Not our works, though, but the works of Christ.
g. So the covenant of grace does not nullify the covenant of works. It fulfills it.
h. These two covenants fit together and fulfill the promises and requirements of God from all eternity.

STUDY QUESTIONS

1. What is the core element of a covenant?
   a. Promise
   b. Oaths
   c. Agreement
   d. Stipulations

2. Who does the covenant of redemption involve?
   a. God and Adam
   b. God and Moses
   c. The triune Godhead
   d. Christ and the church

3. Which covenant describes how God related to human beings before the fall?
   a. The covenant of works
   b. The covenant of grace
   c. The covenant of redemption
   d. The covenant of creation

4. The covenant of works has no element of grace in it.
   a. True
   b. False

5. Which covenant introduces the promise of redemption?
   a. The covenant of redemption
   b. The covenant of works
   c. The covenant of grace
   d. The covenant of salvation

6. By what are we ultimately saved?
   a. By grace
   b. By faith
   c. By our works
   d. By Christ's works

DISCUSSION QUESTIONS

1. What does Hebrews 8:3–6 teach about the new covenant?

2. What is a covenant?

3. What is the covenant of redemption?

4. What is the covenant of works?

5. What is the covenant of grace?

23

The Christ of the Bible

INTRODUCTION

Christology, the doctrine of the person and work of Christ, is foundational for Christian theology. In this lesson, Dr. Sproul paints a picture of the complexities and greatness of Christ as proclaimed from Genesis to Revelation.

MESSAGE OVERVIEW

I. One of the most intimidating sections of theology is Christology.
   a. We must be most careful at this point because Jesus is at the very center of our faith.
   b. It is difficult to summarize God. This problem is compounded with Jesus, as He is richly presented to us in all His splendor throughout Scripture.

II. Some of the most significant passages revealing the glory of Christ are found in Revelation 5.
   a. "Who is worthy to open the scroll and to loose its seals?" No one was found who could do it—until Jesus stepped forward.
   b. This section is skillfully written to produce a sense of expectation. But in the end, John sees a bloody lamb. This profound contrast reveals great humiliation and great exaltation of Christ's life.

III. What has God revealed to us in the gospels concerning Jesus?
   a. God gave us four gospels to give us different perspectives on Jesus' person and ministry.
      i. Matthew
      ii. Mark
      iii. Luke
      iv. John

b. We also see the various responses of people to the person of Christ through these multiple witnesses. The contemporaries of Christ testified to the vastness of His character.
c. Jesus also attested to His own person and origin in the gospels. The "I am" statements of Christ (*Ego emi*) are particularly revealing of His nature.
d. Jesus was more than a perfect man. He was "Immanuel," or "God with us."
e. The Council of Chalcedon said Jesus was, "*Deum verum et hominem verum*"—truly God and truly man. This was so carefully defined because both His natures are so boldly presented.

IV. How do the apostles preach Christ to us?
a. Paul shows how Jesus is our mediator, accomplishing our redemption.
b. The book of Hebrews gives us one of the highest, most beautiful teachings on the person of Christ.

V. How does the Old Testament teach us about Jesus Christ?
a. His person and work are typologically represented in the tabernacle.
b. The prophets are filled with references to the coming Messiah.
c. Christ is preached on virtually every page of the Old Testament.

STUDY QUESTIONS

1. Which field of study concerns the doctrine of Christ?
   a. Theology
   b. Christology
   c. Pneumatology
   d. Soteriology

2. Where do we learn of Christ?
   a. History
   b. Myth
   c. Archaeology
   d. The Bible

3. Revelation 5 depicts Christ's exaltation using which of the following imagery?
   a. As a returning bridegroom
   b. As a sacrificial lamb
   c. As a conquering emperor
   d. As a terrible lion

4. Christ is found only in the New Testament.
   a. True
   b. False

5. What are the two natures of Christ?
   a. His humanity and deity
   b. His humility and exaltation
   c. His partial humanity and partial deity
   d. A mixture of the human and divine natures

6. Who was Jesus Christ?
   a. The Son of God
   b. A great teacher
   c. An upright man
   d. A moral example

DISCUSSION QUESTIONS

1. Why is Christology so difficult or intimidating to teach?

2. In the Bible passages concerning Jesus, which ones present images of Him that you have difficulty accepting?

3. Summarize what we know about Jesus just from the Old Testament.

4. Does the presupposition that the Bible is all about Jesus change the way you read the Bible?

24

The Christ of the Creeds

INTRODUCTION

The early church faced much controversy over the doctrine of Christ. The councils of Nicaea and Chalcedon both aimed to clarify the biblical teaching on Christ's person. In this lesson, Dr. Sproul walks through the controversies over Christ's person and describes Him as both truly God and truly man.

MESSAGE OVERVIEW

I. The greatest concern for the early church was to establish a clear, biblical portrait of Jesus that revealed the unity and diversity of the Godhead.
   a. The various councils during the fourth and fifth centuries are a result of that struggle.
   b. The person of Christ is greatly assaulted during our time.
   c. Throughout its history, the church has had to defend against attacks on the person of Christ similar to those of the Jesus Seminar today.

II. Was the Council of Chalcedon a terminal council?
   a. G.C. Berkouwer, a teacher of Dr. Sproul's at the Free University of Amsterdam, believed it was the last council of church history to define the person of Christ. It was unimaginable that any council could go beyond those statements.
   b. Chalcedon, the fourth ecumenical council (A.D. 451), was brought about because of errors concerning the two natures of Christ.
   c. On the one hand was the error of Eutyches, the promoter of Monophysitism. He taught that the incarnate Christ had only one nature, called a theanthropic nature. It was a hybrid, neither human nor divine.
   d. On the other was the heresy of Nestorius, which was named after him. Nestorius did not deny that Christ had two natures, but he said Jesus also had two distinct personalities. Jesus was actually two persons in his view.

e. Chalcedon said, *Deum verum et hominem verum*. Jesus was truly God and truly man.
f. Four negatives also were established concerning the two natures of Christ.
    i. Without mixture
    ii. Without confusion
    iii. Without separation
    iv. Without division
g. Distinguishing the two natures is not the same as separating them.
h. The mystery of how Christ can be truly God and truly man cannot be penetrated by creeds or reason. It is beyond our full understanding.
i. We can only say so much positively concerning the person of Christ. If you try to think and write beyond Chalcedon, you might as well pick your heresy.
j. Each nature retains its own attributes—a teaching that must not be ignored.

STUDY QUESTIONS

1. What purpose do the creeds of Christ serve?
    a. They set boundaries.
    b. They offer clarity.
    c. They harbor confusion.
    d. They provide protection.

2. What does *Deum verum et hominem verum* mean?
    a. Truly God and truly man
    b. Son of God and Son of man
    c. Word of God made flesh
    d. God's truth and man's truth

3. Which early heresy denied the dual nature of Christ?
    a. Arianism
    b. Nestorianism
    c. Docetism
    d. Eutychianism

4. Which early heresy viewed Christ's two natures as separate personalities?
    a. Arianism
    b. Nestorianism
    c. Docetism
    d. Monophysitism

5. What is the theanthropic nature of Christ?
    a. Love for God
    b. Love for humanity
    c. Hybrid divine human
    d. Deity in human form

6. Which issue provoked the Council of Chalcedon?
   a. The deity of the Holy Spirit
   b. The humanity of Christ
   c. The deity of Christ
   d. The dual nature of Christ

DISCUSSION QUESTIONS

1. What was the main theological goal of the first five centuries?

2. What were the two main heresies confronting the orthodox position on Christ's person?

3. Noting the text of Chalcedon printed below, what questions about Jesus' deity does it answer? What questions remain unanswered?

4. How can the church fight Christological heresy today?

THE CREED OF CHALCEDON

We, then, following the holy fathers, all with one consent teach men to confess one and the same Son, our Lord Jesus Christ, the same perfect in Godhead and also perfect in manhood; truly God and truly man, of a rational soul and body; coessential with the Father according to the Godhead, and consubstantial with us according to the manhood; in all things like unto us, without sin; begotten before all ages of the Father according to the Godhead, and in these latter days, for us and for our salvation, born of the Virgin Mary, the mother of God, according to the manhood; one and the same Christ, Son, Lord, Only-begotten, to be acknowledged in two natures, *without confusion, without change, without division, without separation;* the distinction of natures being by no means taken away by the union, but rather the property of each nature being preserved, and concurring in one person and one subsistence, not parted or divided into two persons, but one and the same Son, and only begotten, God the Word, the Lord Jesus Christ; as the prophets from the beginning have declared concerning Him, and the Lord Jesus Christ Himself has taught us, and the creed of the holy fathers has handed down to us.

25

The Names of Christ

INTRODUCTION

The different titles of Christ in history are descriptive of His character and nature. In this lesson, Dr. Sproul examines the prominent names of Christ found in the New Testament.

MESSAGE OVERVIEW

I. The titles of God are revealing of His character.
   a. At a seminary, a scholar gave an uncharacteristic lecture by reciting the names of Jesus as found in Scripture.
   b. Notice every time the Scripture assigns a title to Jesus.

II. The major titles of Jesus are revealing of His nature.
   a. His most frequent title is "Christ." Notice that "Christ" is not Jesus' last name. Christ means "Messiah" or "the Anointed One."
   b. For Jesus to be the Messiah, He must be the Lamb of God, the Great High Priest, and many other things. Many titles of Jesus interconnect with Messiah.
   c. The title "Lord" got Jesus' followers into a great deal of trouble. This meant that Caesar was not Lord, nor was anyone else. Jesus alone was the Christians' true king, and this claim was at the heart of the persecution of the early church. However, the title also meant "sir."
   d. "Son of Man" is used far less frequently than the other titles. It is Jesus' favorite title for himself, though. All but three of 80 usages are Jesus referring to Himself. But why? It is a designation of a royal deity and judge, as noted in Daniel 7:13.

STUDY QUESTIONS

1. *Christ* is part of Jesus' full name.
   a. True
   b. False

2. Of all of His titles, which title did Jesus most frequently use to refer to Himself?
   a. Christ
   b. Mighty God
   c. Son of Man
   d. Savior

3. What is the Greek word for *Lord*?
   a. *Doulos*
   b. *Christos*
   c. *Kurios*
   d. *Adonai*

4. Which title is representative of the covenant name for Yahweh?
   a. Lord
   b. Lord
   c. God
   d. *Adon*

5. What does *doulos* mean?
   a. Sir
   b. Lord
   c. Slave
   d. Slave owner

6. Which title of Jesus was a challenge to Caesar's authority?
   a. Lord
   b. Prince of Peace
   c. Christ
   d. Immanuel

DISCUSSION QUESTIONS

1. How are the names of Christ theologically significant?

2. What is the most frequently used title of Jesus in Scripture? What does this title mean?

3. What are some of the meanings of the title "Lord"?

4. What title does Jesus use most frequently to refer to Himself? What is the significance of this title?

26

The States of Christ

INTRODUCTION

The states of Christ refer to Christ's role or activity at various times throughout His life and existence. In this lesson, Dr. Sproul covers the states of Christ all the way from His preincarnate existence to His final return.

MESSAGE OVERVIEW

I. The names of Christ, the states of Christ, and the offices of Christ are three ways the Bible discusses the person and work of Jesus.

II. The states of Christ begin not with His birth, but with His pre-incarnate state.
   a. In John 1, John says that Jesus existed prior to His birth. His divine nature is eternally co-existent with the Father.
   b. The Old Testament records several encounters with a being thought to be the pre-incarnate Christ (Josh. 5:13; Ex. 3:2). Such an encounter is called a Christophany.
   c. The Apostles' Creed refers to the birth, death, resurrection, ascension, and final return of Jesus. These are generally known as the states of Christ.

III. The nature of Jesus' states generally flows from humiliation to exaltation.
   a. Jesus is humiliated in His incarnation and daily life, culminating in the Crucifixion, but from that point He experiences greater and greater glory, which will culminate in His return.
   b. This is agreeable up to a point, but has its limits.
   c. In *The Glory of Christ*, Dr. Sproul looked at the manifestations of glory throughout Christ's life. This book shows that Scripture testifies that Christ was always glorious, even in the midst of His pre-resurrection humiliation.

d. A carry-over from His state of humiliation was His physical body. The same body that died came out of the tomb. This reveals that the Incarnation was not completely filled with humiliation, just as the time of humiliation was not devoid of glory.
e. The greatest moment of Christ's glory so far has been the Ascension. (Acts 1). The importance of this event is highly underestimated.
f. Jesus ascended to sit, rule, and intercede on behalf of all believers.
g. It is from this place of majesty that He will return to judge.

STUDY QUESTIONS

1. What was the first state of Christ?
   a. His preincarnate state
   b. His incarnate state
   c. His resurrected state
   d. His glorified state

2. What is a manifestation of the invisible God?
   a. Incarnation
   b. Theophany
   c. Christophany
   d. Anthropomorphism

3. Christ's state of humiliation refers generally to which of the following?
   a. His crucifixion
   b. His burial
   c. His temptation
   d. His incarnation

4. Which moment was Christ's highest point of exaltation?
   a. His virgin conception
   b. His transfiguration
   c. His resurrection
   d. His ascension

5. What do some consider to be the line between Jesus' humiliation and exaltation?
   a. His crucifixion
   b. His ascension
   c. His resurrection
   d. His transfiguration

6. The incarnation was entirely about humiliation.
   a. True
   b. False

DISCUSSION QUESTIONS

1. What are three ways the Bible discusses the person and work of Christ?
2. What biblical passages shed light on the pre-incarnate state of Christ?
3. What are the states of Christ as enumerated in the Apostles' Creed?
4. What do we mean when we speak of the humiliation of Christ?

27

The Offices of Christ

INTRODUCTION

The offices of Christ are connected to Christ's role as mediator. In God's plan for redemption, Christ serves a threefold office called the *munus triplex*. In this lesson, Dr. Sproul explains how Christ fulfills the Old Testament offices as our Prophet, Priest, and King.

MESSAGE OVERVIEW

I. Scholars have chosen to parse the person of Christ in several ways. The richness of His being is not easily summarized in a single formula. One excellent way to understand the person of Christ is to view Him through His offices.
   a. Christ is called our *Mediator*. He is a go-between, someone who stands between two parties. In this case, God and man are in dispute and Jesus is the agent.
   b. There are three kinds of mediators in the Old Testament. They are prophets, priests, and kings.
   c. Christ fulfills all three of the Old Testament offices at once.

II. What is the nature of Jesus' role as prophet?
   a. The prophet was a spokesperson for God, an agent of revelation to mankind. God gave His word to the prophet, then he or she delivered it to the people. The prophet's words were prefaced by the idea, often the words themselves, "Thus saith the Lord."
   b. False prophets often prove attractive to many. God said to Jeremiah that he should not be concerned about false prophets, but should focus on rightly proclaiming God's word.
   c. Jesus was the perfect prophet. Most who met Him immediately knew they were in the presence of a great prophet (John 4). But He did not simply proclaim the word; He was the Word. In this sense, He was the fulfillment of the prophetic ministry.
   d. Jesus was also the object of the prophetic teachings of the Old Testament.

III. How does Jesus fulfill the role of the priest?
   a. What Old Testament passage is quoted most frequently in the New Testament?
   b. Answer: Psalm 110. This incredible prophecy begins, "The Lord said to my Lord. . . ." The book of Hebrews gives much attention to this tremendous passage.
   c. The Old Testament priest came to make intercession for the people, ministering in the most holy of places as he did his work.
   d. In Psalm 110, both ultimate kingship and priesthood are promised to the Messiah.
   e. The writer of Hebrews affirms that Jesus is a greater priest than any other.
   f. Christ's work as priest continues until now as He intercedes for His people at the right hand of the Father.
   g. Just as with Old Testament prophecy, Jesus is the subject and object of the sacrificial system.

IV. Jesus perfectly fulfilled the role of the king.
   a. Jesus manifested the justice and rule of God in a better way than the Old Testament kings. Even though they had been given authority by God, they failed.
   b. We never find a separation of state from God. Church from state, yes. But rulers are accountable to God as to how they exercise their reign. Only God can make a man a ruler.
   c. David is the closest we have to a perfect king. But even his rule makes us long for a perfected version of David. The promise to us is that Jesus is the newly born King of Israel, and His claims to Kingship were what put Him on the cross.
   d. Jesus perfectly fulfills the role of king by wrapping the other offices up into this one. He was a priestly king, a prophetic king, and a kingly king.
   e. Right now, Jesus is the King. He holds the highest office in the universe by being seated at the right hand of God today. There is no other office higher. And He shall reign forever.

STUDY QUESTIONS

1. What is the threefold office of Christ?
   a. Prophet, Judge, and Priest
   b. Prophet, Priest, and King
   c. Priest, Apostle, and King
   d. King, Priest, and Judge

2. What is the title of Christ's role that identifies Him as the One who stands between us and God interceding on our behalf?
   a. Mediator
   b. Minister
   c. Comforter
   d. Prophet

3. Jesus showed Himself to be a prophet by using which phrase?
   a. "Thus saith the Lord"
   b. "In the name of the Lord"
   c. "Truly, I say to you"
   d. "The Lord hath said"

4. To which priesthood does Christ belong?
   a. The Aaronic priesthood
   b. The order of Melchizedek
   c. The Levitical priesthood
   d. The tribe of Judah

5. What kind of king is Christ?
   a. A corrupt king
   b. A shepherd king
   c. A political king
   d. A spiritual king

6. Jesus will not reign as King until He returns and sets up His earthly millennial kingdom.
   a. True
   b. False

DISCUSSION QUESTIONS

1. What are the three kinds of mediators in the Old Testament?

2. How does Jesus fulfill the roles of prophet, priest, and king?

3. How does seeing Him in these roles help explain His work in the economy of God's kingdom?

28

The Substitutionary Atonement

INTRODUCTION

The classical view of Christ's atonement as the substitutionary satisfaction of God's justice is necessary for salvation. In this lesson, Dr. Sproul walks through the different aspects of Christ's atonement found in Scripture.

MESSAGE OVERVIEW

I. The atonement of Christ is one of the most magnificent parts of theology. Anselm's *Cur Deus Homo* or *Why the God/Man?* is one of the most famous works that dealt with Christ's death.

II. The New Testament uses several metaphors to describe the Atonement. It is like a tapestry, with several strands woven through it.
   a. Redemption or purchase
   b. Ransom theories
   c. Bride price
   d. *Christus Victor*
   e. Governmental theories
   f. Satisfaction theory

III. The satisfaction theory gets at the heart of the cause and need of the Atonement.
   a. This theory is based on the justice of God. God's justice is closely related to His righteousness and goodness.
      i. God's justice is perfect.
      ii. Will not the judge of all the world do what is right?
   b. We have both pecuniary and moral debt toward God, as illustrated by the boy in the ice cream shop.
   c. God is both just and the justifier of the ungodly.

STUDY QUESTIONS

1. What does the Greek word *huper* mean?
    a. In lieu of
    b. Because of
    c. On behalf of
    d. Alongside of

2. Which animal was used to symbolize the transfer of one's sin to another on the Day of Atonement?
    a. Bull
    b. Goat
    c. Lamb
    d. Dove

3. What is expiation?
    a. The removal of guilt
    b. The transfer of righteousness
    c. The appeasing of God's wrath
    d. The satisfaction of justice

4. What is the basic question of the atonement?
    a. What do I do with my guilt?
    b. From what am I saved?
    c. How do I receive its benefits?
    d. Why did Christ have to die?

5. What is the covenant curse of sin?
    a. Spiritual death
    b. Pain and suffering
    c. Being cut off from God
    d. Having an inability to be obedient

6. What is the covenant blessing secured for us by Christ's atonement?
    a. The promised land
    b. Victory over our enemies
    c. The presence of God
    d. Riches in heaven

DISCUSSION QUESTIONS

1. List and describe the different theories of the atonement.
2. Why is the satisfaction theory more accurate than the others?
3. Using the Bible's logic, how can God be just and yet be the justifier of sinners who do not deserve mercy?

29

Why Did Christ Die?

INTRODUCTION

Though some consider the notion of substitutionary atonement to be barbaric, it is the only view of the atonement that fully satisfies the demands of God's justice. In this lesson, Dr. Sproul lays out the significance of Christ's death as a substitution and maintains that rejecting the doctrine of penal substitutionary atonement is paramount to rejecting Scripture itself.

MESSAGE OVERVIEW

I. In Dr. Sproul's homiletics class, the teacher would critique the presentation of the student's sermon. But when the substitutionary atonement was preached, he commented on the content.

II. Is the substitutionary atonement a vital part of Christianity? All orthodox (and even some unorthodox) have agreed it is.
   a. Karl Barth said that the most important word in the New Testament was *huper*, or "in behalf of."
   b. Through the First Adam, we all fell. But through the Second Adam, we are redemptively represented. Anselm highlighted this relationship in the previously mentioned *Cur Deus Homo.*

III. Insights from the Old Testament are essential for understanding this aspect of the Atonement.
   a. The Day of Atonement is instructive as to the transfer or imputation of our sins to Christ.
      i. It pointed to the concept of substitution.
      ii. It pointed to the importance of Jesus' very life being given for us, not simply the shedding of His blood.
      iii. Propitiation: horizontal atonement
      iv. Expiation: vertical atonement
      v. What do we do with our guilt?

b. The covenant structure of the Atonement is also revealed in the Old Testament.
   i. Blessing: God's presence
   ii. Cursing: far as the curse is found

IV. Paul makes this aspect of the Atonement clear in Galatians 3:1–14.

STUDY QUESTIONS

1. What does *Cur Deus homo* mean?
   a. "Behold the man!"
   b. "God with us."
   c. "Can Christ be God and man?"
   d. "Why the God-man?"

2. What is central to redemption?
   a. Sacrifice
   b. Purchasing
   c. Blood
   d. Dowery

3. Which ransom theory views mankind as held hostage?
   a. Ransom to the prince
   b. Ransom to Satan
   c. Ransom to the Father
   d. Ransom of the sinner

4. Which view of the atonement sees Christ as the conquering King who defeats His enemies and sets the captives free?
   a. *Christus Victor*
   b. Satisfaction theory
   c. Governmental theory
   d. Ransom theory

5. Which attribute of God is the satisfaction of the atonement largely based upon?
   a. Justice
   b. Love
   c. Sovereignty
   d. Anger

6. Which debt is a monetary debt?
   a. Pecuniary debt
   b. Moral debt
   c. Legal debt
   d. Penal debt

DISCUSSION QUESTIONS

1. What is so offensive about the atonement of Christ?

2. Why is the Atonement a vital part of the Christian faith? What is instructive about the Day of Atonement in its relationship to Jesus' work?

3. What other Old Testament passages reveal aspects of the atonement of Christ?

30

The Extent of the Atonement

INTRODUCTION

The most controversial issue in any discussion of Christ's work as our Savior is the extent of Christ's atonement. In this lesson, Dr. Sproul discusses the subject of limited atonement, also known as definite atonement, in addressing the question, For whom did Christ die?

MESSAGE OVERVIEW

I. One of the most controversial issues surrounding the Atonement is its extent.
   a. The Christmas Calvinist is someone who has "no L."
   b. The L comes from the TULIP acrostic that was developed in Holland in response to the Remonstrants, a group of semi-Pelagian theologians. The L stands for "limited atonement."
   c. Many people believe four points of the acrostic, but reject the L. They may call themselves "Calminians."

II. What is *not* meant by the idea of limited atonement?
   a. The biblical idea of the Atonement is not best summarized by the aforementioned phrase. This problem is inevitable when you reduce a complicated doctrine to two words.
   b. This discussion about Christ's sacrifice is not about its value. The value of the Atonement was infinite, once and for all.
   c. Even some pastors mistakenly say that limited atonement means that Christ's atonement was sufficient for all, but efficient for some. But this description is not sufficient. That Jesus' atonement is not applied efficiently to all people is true for any concept of the Atonement outside of universalism.
   d. Jesus did not die to obtain the possibility of salvation for some. But some evangelicals display a tendency toward universalism by claiming that Jesus

died for everyone in the same way. This creates the unlikely possibility that all will be saved.

e. Salvation is designed, in the Arminian view, in potential or conditional terms. It is the individual's faith that determines the efficiency of the Atonement. Unless you believe, Jesus' work is to no avail.
f. In this view, if Jesus' atonement actually pays for our sin debt to God, and He then sends sinners to hell, God is guilty of punishing the same sins twice. So, for Arminians, God must save only potentially, and not really save anyone from His wrath.

III. How was the Atonement designed?
  a. Who was the designer? God is the planner.
  b. Why did God send Christ to die? Was it to pace up and down heaven's streets, hoping that someone would accept His Son's sacrifice?
  c. With a hypothetical redemption, Jesus can die theoretically for everyone (universalism) and theoretically for nobody (futility).
  d. At a recent meeting of scholars, a well-known Christian leader said that millions of people would be lost without the results of that discussion. Dr. Sproul disagreed.
  e. Is salvation of man or of God? Jesus said, "I lay down my life for My sheep." This does not sound potential at all.
  f. In one sense, the offer of the Gospel is not universal. The promises of the Gospel are only offered to the believing, repentant sinner. God enables such a response (and thus enables us to meet His conditions), and so it is accurate to say that the Gospel is offered only to those who respond in faith.
  g. If the Gospel offer is not universal, then can the atonement of Christ be universal? Every person for whom Christ dies is saved. Jesus died only for the elect.
  h. But what about the passages that say Jesus died for the world? Those have been misinterpreted by those from the semi-Pelagian perspective to mean Jesus died for every single person in a potential way. This is reading far too much into those passages. They seem to refer only to the racial reality of the Atonement—that Jesus also died for non-Jews. Jesus died for Gentiles.
  i. Did Jesus die for Satan or other fallen angels? No. But we accept this limit to the Atonement quite easily. Jesus did not die for those who were not God's special objects of favor.

IV. How can someone embrace four points of Calvinism and not embrace limited atonement?
  a. Total depravity, rightly understood, makes particular atonement absolutely necessary.
  b. Unconditional election, rightly understood, makes particular atonement absolutely necessary.

c. The five points of Calvinism need to be taken as a group, for they cannot be logically held separately.
d. The Cross is a part of God's eternal plan of redemption. It was His intention that Christ not die in vain but that He accomplish His goal: to save the elect.

STUDY QUESTIONS

1. What is a better way to word "limited atonement"?
   a. Sufficient for all, efficient for some
   b. Definite atonement
   c. Indefinite atonement
   d. Conditional atonement

2. The Reformed view holds that Christ's atonement was designed and intended for which of the following?
   a. For all men
   b. For Christ Himself
   c. Only for the elect
   d. Only for national Israel

3. What does Scripture mean when it says Christ died once "for all" the world?
   a. All individual people of the world
   b. All peoples all around the world
   c. All nonelect
   d. All mankind

4. Belief in hell makes which of the following theological views obsolete?
   a. Particularism
   b. Universalism
   c. Arminianism
   d. Hypothetical Universalism

5. The doctrine of limited atonement teaches that Jesus died to make salvation ________.
   a. Possible
   b. Available
   c. Potential
   d. Actual

6. What doctrine of grace do "four-point Calvinists" usually reject?
   a. Predestination
   b. Limited atonement
   c. Unconditional election
   d. Providence

DISCUSSION QUESTIONS

1. What is Dr. Sproul's critique of unlimited or universal atonement? How is universal atonement different from the doctrine of universalism (all will be saved)? How is it similar?

2. Briefly, what is Dr. Sproul's argument for the necessity of a particular atonement? What problems does this position solve? What encouragements does this position give? What are some objections to it? How does Dr. Sproul answer them?

3. What are the problems with believing some points of Calvinism without embracing a particular atonement?

31

The Holy Spirit in the Old Testament

INTRODUCTION

Most people are confused by the work of the Holy Spirit in the lives of the Old Testament saints. In this lesson, Dr. Sproul begins a study of the person and work of the Holy Spirit by looking at His work within the context of the Old Testament, confirming His role in empowering individuals to carry out particular functions on behalf of God.

MESSAGE OVERVIEW

I. What are the significant events in your life?
   a. Dr. Sproul's conversion was very significant. He was engaged to a woman who thought he had gone crazy when he was converted. But when she was converted, one of her first comments was, "Now I know who the Holy Spirit is!"
   b. Notice the pronoun choice: "who," not "what."

II. Who is the Holy Spirit?
   a. The Holy Spirit has a will, knowledge, and affections, all of which add up to His being a person.
   b. A point of confusion is the manifestation of the Holy Spirit in Old Testament times as compared to the New.

III. Genesis 1:2 says that the Spirit hovered over the waters. This begins our understanding of God the Holy Spirit in the Old Testament.
   a. The gap theory does not help us at this point.
   b. Carl Sagan, on the first page of his book "Cosmos," makes a point of saying that we live in a cosmos, not a chaotic universe. What we have in Genesis 1 is a proclamation of God's oversight, via the Holy Spirit, of all that was made.
   c. The overwhelming power of God that is manifested in the Old Testament narratives is focused through the Holy Spirit. He is the *dunamis* (power) of God.

d. The offices of the prophet, priest, and king were all charismatic offices, that is, empowered, gifted or anointed by the Holy Spirit. That the Holy Spirit could anoint or empower someone to do a certain task did not necessarily mean that he had been regenerated by the Spirit. Gifted, yes, but not internally changed.

STUDY QUESTIONS

1. When is the first time the Holy Spirit appears in the Old Testament?
   a. At creation
   b. After Abel's death
   c. During the flood
   d. During the exodus

2. What is the meaning behind the word *dunamis?*
   a. Power
   b. Majesty
   c. Honor
   d. Glory

3. In the Old Testament, how did the Holy Spirit prepare men for the offices of prophet, priest, and king?
   a. He prompted them.
   b. He tempted them.
   c. He accepted them.
   d. He anointed them.

4. The Holy Spirit filled all of God's people in the Old Testament.
   a. True
   b. False

5. Who informed Moses that sharing the job of leadership with gifted elders was a wise idea?
   a. Aaron
   b. Miriam
   c. Joshua
   d. Jethro

6. Who does the Bible first speak of being filled with the Holy Spirit?
   a. The craftsmen
   b. The judges
   c. The prophets
   d. The musicians

DISCUSSION QUESTIONS

1. What are some biblical passages that indicate the personhood of the Holy Spirit?
2. What does Genesis 1 teach us about the Holy Spirit?
3. What is the primary difference between the work of the Holy Spirit in the Old Testament and the New?

32

The Holy Spirit in the New Testament

INTRODUCTION

It is by the Holy Spirit that the redemptive work of Christ is applied to the believer. It is through His work that they are granted spiritual life. In this lesson, Dr. Sproul continues his study of the Holy Spirit by looking at His work within the context of the New Testament, particularly in the work of regeneration.

MESSAGE OVERVIEW

I. God did not create humans as empty sculptures. We were given "spirits." God breathes into us His own life. The Holy Spirit is the genesis of life. In a broad sense, no one is conceived by anything other than the Holy Spirit.

II. The word for "spirit" in Hebrew and Greek is linked to breath and wind.
   a. When Jesus says He comes to give life to others, He is saying that He will give them spiritual life.
   b. In the New Testament, we see a new genesis described in depth: regeneration.

III. The New Testament uncovers more of the internal workings of the Spirit.
   a. The Spirit regenerates us.
   b. In Ephesians 2, the Bible teaches that people are not all beloved by God; we are born enemies of God.
   c. This teaching from Ephesians 2 is quite surprising to many in the church today. But the Holy Spirit is intimately involved in making enemies of God His friends.
   d. John 3 is clear on the necessity of the Spirit's work in the life of a believer.
   e. There are no non-born again Christians. We must experience rebirth by the Spirit (John 3:5).
   f. Why is the Spirit designated as holy?

g. The Holy Spirit inspired the original record of Scripture. But now He helps us understand the nature of Scripture. He illumines it for us.

STUDY QUESTIONS

1. The Greek and Hebrew words for "spirit" are connected to which English words?
    a. Breath and wind
    b. Force and power
    c. Life and energy
    d. Ghost and specter
2. What does the Holy Spirit give in His direct involvement in creation and redemption?
    a. Revelation
    b. Love
    c. Life
    d. Wisdom
3. The Spirit is called "holy" because He is intimately involved in making God's people holy.
    a. True
    b. False
4. What term refers to the Spirit's assistance in helping us understand and apply Scripture?
    a. Illumination
    b. Inspiration
    c. Indoctrination
    d. Sanctification
5. What term refers to the Holy Spirit's work of imparting new life to dead souls?
    a. Baptism
    b. Adoption
    c. Sanctification
    d. Regeneration
6. How were people saved in the Old Testament?
    a. By keeping the law
    b. By offering sacrifices
    c. By obeying God
    d. By regeneration

DISCUSSION QUESTIONS

1. How is the Holy Spirit involved in the creation of the universe? Of individual humans? Of new believers?

2. Why is the Spirit designated as "holy"?

3. How is the Spirit involved with the creation and reading of Scripture?

33

The Paraclete

INTRODUCTION

The Holy Spirit plays a vital role in the lives of believers and in the life of the church. He is the Paraclete, the Helper whom Christ promised to send. In this lesson, Dr. Sproul explains the importance of the Spirit's role as the promised Comforter whom God has sent to be with His people in the midst of a hostile world.

MESSAGE OVERVIEW

I. In John 15, Jesus discusses hatred. This may be surprising, but it is a discussion of the world's hatred of Him.
    a. If the world hates Me, the world will hate you.
    b. I will send you a Comforter.
    c. Who is the *Paraclete*? It is not exactly correct to say that the *Paraclete* is the only *Paraclete*—Jesus was the first.

II. The idea of the Paraclete has been associated with comfort.
    a. Frederick Nietzsche assaulted the idea of a living God, let alone a God who is with us as a comforter.
    b. Our idea of a comforter and the nature of the Holy Spirit's comfort can be quite different.
    c. *Paraclete* means "to call someone alongside." In Greek culture, this referred to a family attorney who was kept on retainer. Older translations use the word "advocate," which is a good translation.
    d. If we follow the term *comfort* back in its history, we discover that it is a good translation as well. It developed from two words that meant "with" and "strength." This takes us further away from viewing the Holy Spirit as a simple caregiver.

e. We are conquerors, developed and strengthened by the Holy Spirit through the application of truth.
f. In the Upper Room Discourse, we learn more about the Holy Spirit than in any other section of the Bible.

STUDY QUESTIONS

1. The Holy Spirit is the only Paraclete mentioned in Scripture.
   a. True
   b. False

2. What is the original meaning for the word *comforter*?
   a. With solace
   b. With sympathy
   c. With sacrifice
   d. With strength

3. What is the example of a paraclete from ancient Greek culture?
   a. The family lawyer
   b. The family doctor
   c. A family friend
   d. A family dog

4. Which of the following does the Upper Room Discourse tell us more about than does the rest of the New Testament combined?
   a. The Holy Spirit
   b. The Father
   c. The Son
   d. The Disciples

5. Which nineteenth-century philosopher despised the idea of meekness?
   a. Fyodor Dostoevsky
   b. Friedrich Nietzsche
   c. Immanuel Kant
   d. Jean-Jacques Rousseau

6. What is the final teaching session Jesus had with His disciples before the crucifixion?
   a. The Sermon on the Mount
   b. The Sermon on the Plain
   c. The Olivet Discourse
   d. The Upper Room Discourse

DISCUSSION QUESTIONS

1. What do we mean by the term *Paraclete*?

2. Who was the first *Paraclete*?

3. What passage of the New Testament gives us the greatest amount of insight into the work of the Holy Spirit?

34

The Baptism of the Holy Spirit

INTRODUCTION

Have you been asked, "Are you baptized in the Holy Spirit?" What does that mean? In this lesson, Dr. Sproul discusses "the baptism of the Holy Spirit," as well as the related phenomenon of speaking in tongues and the false distinction between conversion and baptism in the Spirit.

MESSAGE OVERVIEW

I. The Charismatic movement has had an incredible impact on the church.
   a. What are the roots of the movement?
   b. What is the baptism of the Holy Spirit?
   c. The baptism of the Holy Spirit and speaking in tongues originally were linked to a perfectionistic view of sanctification.

II. The history and doctrine of the baptism of the Holy Spirit is rooted in Wesleyan perfectionism.
   a. Originally, it was an experience that marked your perfection. The sign that accompanied it was speaking in tongues.
   b. This doctrine began to come over into different denominations. But how do you integrate this doctrine with historic Christianity?
   c. Neo-Pentecostalism was the result. The baptism was seen in this movement as the sign of a supernatural gifting of God. Neo-Pentecostals disagree over the sign of tongues.
   d. But they do agree that there is a time gap between conversion and the reception of the baptism. The body of Christ is split between the have's and the have not's.
   e. The basis for this view of the doctrine is the Acts narrative.

III. The biblical record in Acts must be the basis of our acceptance or rejection of this doctrine.
   a. What do the events of Pentecost (Acts 2) mean?
   b. There were all sorts of visible and audible signs during Pentecost. When Peter interprets these events, he quotes a passage from Joel.
   c. The gifts of the Spirit no longer will be limited to prophets, priests, kings, and a few others.
   d. This interpretation makes it hard to argue that this baptism is only for some believers. Joel makes it clear that the baptism or gifting of believers was to be for all people everywhere, not just a few.
   e. The Jewish believers at Pentecost all received this new gifting. Not just some, all.

IV. There are three other mini-Pentecosts in Acts.
   a. Non-Jews received this gifting in these situations found in Acts 8, 10, and 19.
   b. These outpourings have suggested a permanent separation between conversion and gifting.

V. As the Gospel was preached to these various groups, the question of whether these people were "real" Christians naturally arose.
   a. Luke says "yes" by tracing the expansion of the Gospel through its victories in those from "Jerusalem, Judea, Samaria, and the uttermost parts of the earth."
   b. Paul says, "Were we not all baptized by one Spirit?" in reference to these Pentecostal events. All Christians are given these gifts, not just a few.

STUDY QUESTIONS

1. The Pentecostal view of the baptism of the Holy Spirit was originally linked to what teaching?
   a. Perfectionism
   b. Moralism
   c. Adoptionism
   d. Legalism

2. At Pentecost, the Apostles declared the gifts of the Holy Spirit would fall on certain anointed members of the church.
   a. True
   b. False

3. There is no time gap between which salvation reality and the baptism of the Holy Spirit?
   a. Justification
   b. Sanctification
   c. Adoption
   d. Regeneration

4. What do the "mini-Pentecosts" throughout the book of Acts demonstrate?
   a. Gospel exclusion
   b. Gospel exception
   c. Gospel expansion
   d. Gospel existence

5. What was the primary issue as the gospel was received by the gentiles?
   a. Whether the gentiles had full membership rights
   b. Whether the gentiles should be circumcised
   c. Whether the gentiles could be saved
   d. Whether the gentiles could associate with Jews

6. What was Moses' desire for the people of Israel?
   a. That they would trust and obey God
   b. That they would receive the Holy Spirit
   c. That they would stop murmuring
   d. That they would enter the promised land

DISCUSSION QUESTIONS

1. How did the Wesleyan movement understand the baptism of the Holy Spirit?

2. How do charismatics understand the baptism of the Holy Spirit?

3. How does Peter's use of Joel in Acts shed light on the baptism of the Holy Spirit?

4. What is the significance of the three mini-Pentecosts in Acts?

35

The Gifts of the Spirit

INTRODUCTION

Christ has given the church gifts of the Holy Spirit to edify and strengthen the entire body. In the lesson, Dr. Sproul explores the different views of spiritual gifts and examines the validity of spiritual gifts in the context of our day.

MESSAGE OVERVIEW

I. Why has more been written on the Holy Spirit in the last fifty years than in the two thousand previous?
   a. The charismatic movement has had a great impact on Protestantism and Catholicism.
   b. The subject of tongues and the broader question of the gifts of the Spirit have become popular and academic areas of interest.

II. Is the "speaking in tongues" in Acts the same thing that happened to the church at Corinth?
   a. At Pentecost, the miracle was not so much in the speaking as in the hearing. There was a miracle of translation, not a production of languages. But there is no explicit teaching of this in Acts, so we must not speculate too strongly.
   b. In Corinth, we see that there is a miracle of language. But that miracle is not uniformly reproduced in church history. The manifestation of tongues has varied in almost every way throughout history, which brings into question whether the event in Corinth is the baseline for the continuance of what we think of as "the gift of tongues."
   c. Is the revival of tongues a sign of the "latter rain"?
   d. Was the tongues speaking in Corinth miraculous, or a natural and permitted event?

III. The most lengthy discussion of spiritual gifts in scripture is in 1 Corinthians 12–14.
   a. One of the most popular chapters in the Bible is 1 Corinthians 13. In the midst of his discussion of spiritual gifts, Paul writes a poetic and powerful dissertation on love. This must be the basis for the use of the gifts.
   b. In 1 Corinthians 12, Paul begins by stating he does not want people to be ignorant about spiritual gifts.
   c. At the end of the first century, Clement writes the Corinthians and reminds them of Paul's letters, encouraging them to obey them. They were still struggling with misuse of the gifts, among other problems.
   d. In 1 Corinthians 12:1–10, Paul lists various manifestations of the Holy Spirit present in the church. There is no reason to believe this is an exhaustive list. These gifts are diverse.
   e. 1 Corinthians 12:11–13 discusses the baptism of the Holy Spirit. Here Paul teaches that all Christians have been baptized by the Holy Spirit, contradicting Pentecostal teachings. Also, he shows that the entire body has been equipped to minister, not just a designated few. The priesthood of all believers, which is clearly taught here, was emphasized by the Reformers.
   f. 1 Corinthians 12:14–26 illustrates the need to allow this diversity to exist without limiting it or emphasizing one gift over the other.
   g. Paul then goes on to list offices and gifts in the church, putting tongues last. Some are called "best gifts" and apostleship is demonstrated to be a more important office.

IV. In 1 Corinthians 14, Paul revisits his straightforward teaching concerning the gifts.
   a. In what sense is Paul using the word "prophesy" here?
   b. In verses 4–6, Paul seems to clearly designate the tongues in Corinth as different from those in Acts.
   c. Focusing on verse 6, tongues then and now were unintelligible. But they do not necessarily seem to be supernatural, but a natural event of religious ecstasy. Today, people may be speaking in tongues, and this speaking may be speaking with God, but it does not require miraculous enabling any more than normal prayer does.
   d. Tongues takes place in many religions. There is no discernible difference between the various religious, ecstatic expressions in Mormonism or Catholicism and the experience of Christians who speak in tongues. They sound the same.
   e. Paul goes on in verses 6–19 to show how this gift is to be used. The accent is on order, not disorder.
   f. Tongues are not bad, but according to Paul, prophecy is better.
   g. The warning for us is that we not exalt this particular gift as a sign of spirituality. It is not a sign of special empowerment of God.

STUDY QUESTIONS

1. What was the nature of the miracle at Pentecost, according to Dr. Sproul?
   a. A speaking miracle
   b. A healing miracle
   c. A prophesying miracle
   d. A hearing miracle

2. The gift of tongues that occurred at Corinth has uniform continuity throughout church history.
   a. True
   b. False

3. The priesthood of all believers is emphasized by the fact that spiritual gifts are given to whom?
   a. The whole church
   b. The whole world
   c. The whole priesthood
   d. The whole nation

4. The Apostle Paul said that speaking in tongues is good, but what is better?
   a. Healing
   b. Miracle working
   c. Preaching
   d. Prophecy

5. Which gift should believers pursue above all other gifts?
   a. Service
   b. Prophecy
   c. Tongues
   d. Love

6. What is the primary function of the gift of prophecy?
   a. To predict the future
   b. To explain God's truth
   c. To deliver new revelation
   d. To write Scripture

DISCUSSION QUESTIONS

1. Are the "tongues" in Acts identical to the "tongues" in 1 Corinthians? Defend your answer.

2. What is the evidence that the miracle at Pentecost was a miracle of hearing? What is the evidence against this position?

3. What is the evidence that the gift of tongues in 1 Corinthians is a language miracle? What is the evidence against this position?

4. In what passage of Scripture do we find the most information about spiritual gifts?

5. Have all Christians been baptized by the Holy Spirit? Explain.

36

The Fruit of the Spirit

INTRODUCTION

The chief goal of the Holy Spirit is to apply the gospel in such a way as to fulfill the will of God. In this lesson, Dr. Sproul details and describes the fruit of the Spirit so that we as Christians might know how to pursue it in our lives.

MESSAGE OVERVIEW

I. The church has always struggled with the proper use of the spiritual gifts because of the human penchant for the extraordinary.
   a. The fruit of the Holy Spirit is much more important than the gifts.
   b. One can be very gifted, but be immature and cause great damage in the church.

II. In Galatians 5, Paul teaches concerning the importance of the fruit of the Spirit. But he begins by discussing the fruit of the flesh.
   a. Starting in verse 16, he says that we are to walk in the Spirit. There is no shortcut on the path to maturity.
   b. Paul contrasts flesh and spirit in verse 17. The Greek words *sarx* and *soma* are terms denoting the English word *body*. But *sarx* is used often to denote the metaphysical body, the sinful flesh. This is the use of "flesh" in Galatians 5.
   c. Paul contrasts the fruit of the Spirit with the fruit of the flesh (19–21).
   d. One of the most frightening passages in the Bible: "Those who practice such things will not inherit the kingdom of God" (Gal. 5:21). What does "practice" mean in this context?

III. The fruit of the Spirit are in contrast to the fruit of the flesh.
   a. What do you want on your tombstone?
   b. Notice the difference between the fruit and the gifts of the Spirit. The fruit of the Spirit are to be manifested by all Christians.

c. Our understanding of these fruit is lacking. For instance, meekness is maligned as weakness. Actually, meekness is having power but choosing to be gracious.
d. Gentleness is associated with meekness, as it implies tenderness toward those who are weak and helpless. A gentle person is strong against the strong, but careful with the broken ones.
e. Joy is more than not being a sourpuss. It does not preclude experiencing pain or sadness. It is an overarching attitude of happiness at being chosen by God.
f. Longsuffering is related to patience.
g. These fruits imitate the character of God. It is God who is the source of the fruit of the Christian life.
h. Kindness is somewhat difficult to explain, but we know it through experience—you know when someone is nice to you or mean to you.
i. Production of these fruits keeps us from grieving the Holy Spirit, whose goal it is to sanctify us.

STUDY QUESTIONS

1. The fruit of the Holy Spirit corresponds to one's gifting in the Holy Spirit.
   a. True
   b. False

2. What does the Greek word *sarx* mean?
   a. Flesh
   b. Spirit
   c. Soul
   d. Nature

3. What is a proper synonym for the word *meek*?
   a. Weak
   b. Gentle
   c. Gracious
   d. Winsome

4. Why should we cultivate the fruit of the Holy Spirit?
   a. To avoid blaspheming the Spirit
   b. To avoid thwarting the Spirit
   c. To avoid frustrating the Spirit
   d. To avoid grieving the Spirit

5. What is the primary mandate that the Scriptures give us concerning the Holy Spirit?
   a. To walk in the Spirit
   b. To prophecy in the Spirit
   c. To speak in the Spirit
   d. To heal in the Spirit

6. What is long-suffering related to?
   a. Joy
   b. Love
   c. Kindness
   d. Patience

DISCUSSION QUESTIONS

1. What biblical passage enumerates the fruit of the Spirit? What is the fruit of the Spirit?

2. What are the differences between the fruit of the Spirit and the gifts of the Spirit?

3. What is the difference between the Greek words *sarx* and *soma*?

4. What is the meaning of the word “practice” in Galatians 5:21?

37

Are Miracles for Today?

INTRODUCTION

In the church today, miracles are a subject of debate. Should we expect miracles to occur in the contemporary church, or did miracles cease at the end of the Apostolic age? In this lesson, Dr. Sproul explains in detail some of the issues surrounding the question of whether miracles occur today.

MESSAGE OVERVIEW

I. The topic of the person and work of the Holy Spirit has several controversial questions connected to it. One of the most interesting is the nature of modern miracles.
    a. Did miracles end with the close of the apostolic age?
    b. Can Satan and his minions perform miracles?
    c. Most people think miracles do continue in the church today and they believe Satan can do miracles. But Dr. Sproul disagrees.

II. Those who do not believe in the occurrence of miracles today, by Satan or anyone else, hold a position that is frequently misunderstood.
    a. What is a miracle? Is it any supernatural work, or can it be something like the birth of a baby?
    b. "Expect a miracle" is not an appropriate saying because if they were ordinary and expected they would not be unexpected. Miracles in the Bible were concentrated around certain people, but these flurries of miracles were often hundreds of years apart.
    c. The Greek and Hebrew languages do not have direct correspondents to the word *miracle*. The concept we study in theology is one that is taken from three different words.
        i. Signs, powers, and wonders
        ii. John's favorite word for *miracle* was *sign* because it signified some-

thing important in Christ's teaching. See John 3, the story of Nicodemus, as an example. Also see Hebrews 2.

iii. The point is that if an agent of revelation uses signs to prove his words are from God, what happens to that proof if another person, such as the devil, can duplicate those signs? The original proof would not mean anything.

iv. What about those who stand in churches or arenas and proclaim that they are about to perform miracles? If they are performing true miracles, then we need to heed what they say and write down every word as true.

v. For these reasons, theologians have given a very tight definition of miracle. In a broad sense, God has an ongoing supernatural activity in His church. But in a narrow sense, a miracle is an extraordinary work performed by the immediate power of God in the external, perceivable world. It is an act against nature that only God can do, such as bringing life out of death or something out of nothing. We do not see these events happening today.

vi. Christ was confirmed in His Sonship by the Resurrection.

vii. If Satan can do miracles, how do we know the Resurrection was not done by Satan? As terrible as it is to ask this question, how do we know that Satan did not miraculously support the ministry of Jesus Christ, make Him appear to be the Messiah, and lead all God's people astray for two thousand years by this deception? We know because Satan cannot do miracles.

viii. What is a lying sign or wonder? Is it a real miracle or a fake one? It is a fake, an untrue trick.

d. Satan can be very clever, but do not give him the ability to do things that only God can do.

STUDY QUESTIONS

1. Which of the following is not a biblical term?
   a. Wonder
   b. Sign
   c. Power
   d. Miracle

2. What does the presence of miracles authenticate?
   a. Regeneration
   b. Repentance
   c. Revelation
   d. Resurrection

3. What was the resurrection a confirmation of?
   a. That Jesus was the Son of God
   b. That death had been defeated
   c. That sin had been paid for
   d. That the new age had dawned

4. The devil can do miracles.
   a. True
   b. False

5. What is a miracle?
   a. A mediate act of God's providence
   b. An immediate act of God's power
   c. God's answers to prayer
   d. An action that is out of the ordinary

6. How did the Reformers respond to Rome's accusation of not having any miracles?
   a. They presented their own miracles.
   b. They pointed to the miracles of the Apostles.
   c. They couldn't give any examples.
   d. They argued the proper definition of miracle.

DISCUSSION QUESTIONS

1. Explain the biblical arguments behind the position that affirms Satanic miracles and the occurrence of miracles in the church today.

2. What is the problem with this position? Explain the opposite position, which is held by Dr. Sproul. Which do you think is right?

3. The Bible teaches that Satan and his followers can do false signs. Are these real miracles? What is the narrow definition of a miracle?

38

Common Grace

INTRODUCTION

According to the classic definition, grace is unmerited or unearned favor. In this lesson, Dr. Sproul builds on this understanding and makes the important distinction between common (universal) grace and special (salvific) grace.

MESSAGE OVERVIEW

I. Another subdivision of theology is soteriology: a summary of the message of salvation as taught in Scripture.
   a. Salvation is seen as rescue from calamity.
   b. Grace is at the heart of soteriology.

II. The contrast between grace and justice is plain, but crucial.
   a. Justice has to do with works and falling short of some standard of merit.
   b. Grace is unearned and God is never obligated to deliver it (Rom. 9).
   c. Grace is unmerited favor.

III. The distinction between common grace and special grace is not as clear, but crucial.
   a. Common grace is given to all in a broad sense. God providentially causes the rain to fall on the just and the unjust. God preserves His creation, and this is part of His ordinary grace.
   b. Christianity has had a powerful positive effect on the world.
   c. In the past century, men and women began to deny historic Christianity. But they didn't want to be out of a job, so they focused on dispensing common grace, caring for the sick and poor. This amounted to a denial of special grace. But we should not ignore either of God's gifts.

IV. In common grace matters, can we be co-belligerents with non-Christians?
   a. In arenas of common grace, we join with those who have similar concerns.
   b. In arenas of special grace, such as a worship service, we remain separate.

V. "Jacob have I loved, but Esau have I hated."
   - God's love of benevolence is key to understanding verses such as these.

STUDY QUESTIONS

1. What does soteriology study?
   a. Sin
   b. Society
   c. Sacraments
   d. Salvation

2. What is grace?
   a. Unabated power
   b. Unmerited favor
   c. Unconditional love
   d. Unilateral mercy

3. The church should focus exclusively on areas of common grace, such as feeding the poor.
   a. True
   b. False

4. What is the name given to God's general love towards all mankind?
   a. Complacency
   b. Indulgence
   c. Benevolence
   d. Toleration

5. What stimulated interest in bettering the human condition?
   a. The sciences
   b. The government
   c. The philosophers
   d. The church

6. What is God's love of complacency?
   a. God's concern for all humans
   b. God's love for His Son
   c. God's care for creation
   d. God's love for the church

DISCUSSION QUESTIONS

1. What is the difference between grace and justice?
2. What is common grace? How is it distinguished from special grace?
3. How does the doctrine of common grace affect our evaluation of modern cultural issues?

39

Election and Reprobation

INTRODUCTION

When trying to understand God's decrees, believers come face-to-face with the difficult doctrine of predestination. In this lesson, Dr. Sproul explores many of the challenging questions that arise when we consider the relationship between salvation and the sovereign decrees of God.

MESSAGE OVERVIEW

I. The doctrine of election is either the heart or heartburn of the church.
   a. This doctrine is open to many distortions and must be treated with great care.
   b. Ephesians 1 makes it clear that predestination is not something that was created by Augustine or Calvin. Serious students of the Bible must have some doctrine of election.
   c. Election is done to the praise of God's grace. It is a glorious thing.
   d. "To choose beforehand" or "to select" are behind the Greek terms sprinkled throughout the Scriptures in relation to God's objects of special favor.
   e. Election means that God has contemplated the mass of fallen humanity and has decreed to save some of those sinful people. To the rest, He distributes His just punishment. He is not fair—fair would mean punishing everyone.

II. Romans 9 is one of the key passages that explain election.
   a. Paul refers back to the entire history of redemption to prove his point about election. Specifically, he focuses on Abraham and his descendants.
   b. God selected prior to any good or bad works.
   c. The foreknowledge doctrine of election (or prescience view) is that God looks at our works and elects based on who will say yes or no to the Gospel.
   d. Does the doctrine of election mean that God is unrighteous?

e. If Paul was teaching foreknowledge election, why would anyone assume that this would make God unrighteous? This is one of many critical blows to the prescience position.
f. It is not of him who wills or runs, but of God who shows mercy.
g. Election is also reprobation: God's decree concerning the non-elect. Is predestination double or single?
h. Predestination is "double or nothing." But which view?
    i. Positive-positive
    ii. Positive-negative
i. Nobody gets injustice. But some get mercy and some get justice.

STUDY QUESTIONS

1. What phrase is the most accurate in summarizing the doctrine of election?
    a. To love beforehand
    b. To choose beforehand
    c. To know beforehand
    d. To summon beforehand

2. How did God select people in relation to their good or bad works?
    a. Prior to their good or bad works
    b. Simultaneous with their good or bad works
    c. Subsequent to their good or bad works
    d. Contrary to their good or bad works

3. What view of predestination holds that God chooses whom He will save based on His foreknowledge of who will choose Him?
    a. Infralapsarianism
    b. Supralapsarianism
    c. Double predestination
    d. Prescient predestination

4. The prescient view of election can reasonably be used to question God's justice.
    a. True
    b. False

5. What does the doctrine of reprobation seek to understand?
    a. Whether God chooses some for condemnation
    b. Whether God chooses some to be sinners
    c. Whether God chooses to condemn believers
    d. Whether God chooses to justify sinners

6. What question does a correct understanding of predestination raise?
    a. Is there injustice in God?
    b. Is there goodness in man?
    c. Is there purpose in the atonement?
    d. Is the free offer of the gospel legitimate?

DISCUSSION QUESTIONS

1. What is the definition of election?

2. What are two of the key New Testament passages that shed light on the doctrine of election?

3. What is the foreknowledge view of election?

4. Why is the foreknowledge view of election difficult to explain in the light of the objections Paul anticipates to his doctrine?

40

Effectual Calling

INTRODUCTION

What is it that God does when He intervenes in a person's life to bring them to faith? In this lesson, Dr. Sproul addresses this important question as he distinguishes between the views of monergism and synergism. Is it God alone who changes the heart of the sinner, or does this change of heart rest also on the willingness of the sinner?

MESSAGE OVERVIEW

I. The sovereignty of divine grace makes necessary a discussion of exactly what God does to draw someone to himself.
   a. Augustine and Pelagius continue to have their representatives in our time as both sides try to explain how someone comes to Christ.
   b. To what degree is grace necessary? Is the sinner's first step of turning from death to life accomplished monergistically or synergistically?
   c. Monergism means "work alone" or "one worker."
   d. Synergism means "co-operation."
   e. Does the Holy Spirit add His power to our own, or is regeneration a unilateral work of God?

II. Ephesians 2:1–10 makes it clear that God is giving spiritual life to dead men.
   a. Dead people don't co-operate. Lazarus was not invited to come out of the tomb—he was commanded. Then, he co-operated.
   b. God proves His rich mercy and love by saving dead men.
   c. We are justified through faith, but faith is not something we generate. Dead people don't have faith.
   d. Unless we are born again (regenerate), we cannot enter the kingdom of God.
   e. A key difference between Reformed theology and many others is that most believe that faith precedes regeneration. But since the days of Paul, the

church has been arguing that regeneration precedes faith. You cannot persuade a dead man to live. You can't change people's hearts, and neither can they change their own.

f. Who chooses Christ, then? Does God choose for us?

III. Grace is a necessary part of salvation. But is it effectual or irresistible?

a. Do dead people struggle? Do dead people resist? The Arminian view does not take seriously the deadness of the nature of man.

b. Why do some become believers while others do not? Are some more righteous than others? Are some smarter? If God has left salvation up to us, then some are clearly superior to others. The Christian has reason to boast, counter to Ephesians 2:8–9.

c. Romans 8:28–30 teaches that there is a chain, a series of logical events, which take place in all those who are saved. All who are internally called by the Holy Spirit are eventually glorified.

STUDY QUESTIONS

1. What does the word *monergism* mean?
   a. "One worker"
   b. "Together with"
   c. "Alongside of"
   d. "On behalf of"

2. Faith precedes regeneration in the order of salvation.
   a. True
   b. False

3. What example did Dr. Sproul use to illustrate effectual calling?
   a. Abraham
   b. Moses
   c. Lazarus
   d. Paul

4. What is effectual calling sometimes referred to as?
   a. Total depravity
   b. Unconditional election
   c. Limited atonement
   d. Irresistible grace

5. When people say that they chose God, what is the attitude underlying their thinking?
   a. That they are more righteous than some
   b. That they are more spiritual than some
   c. That they are more blessed than some
   d. That they are more resolute than some

6. Everyone who is called is also ______.
   a. Justified
   b. Sanctified
   c. Glorified
   d. Predestined

DISCUSSION QUESTIONS

1. What is the definition of "monergism"?

2. What is the definition of "synergism"?

3. Does regeneration precede faith or does faith precede regeneration? Explain.

4. Define effectual grace.

41

Justification by Faith Alone

INTRODUCTION

The doctrine of justification by faith is so significant that it provoked the Protestant Reformation of the sixteenth century. In this lesson, Dr. Sproul defines justification and its necessary components.

MESSAGE OVERVIEW

I. Luther called election the heart of the church. But he is known primarily as the recoverer of *sola fide*, justification by faith alone.
   a. The formal cause of the Reformation was the authority of the church, but the material cause was justification.
   b. The doctrine of justification answers the question: What must I do to be saved?

II. The divine justice of God seems to argue against a doctrine of justification at all.
   a. You can't simply work harder (legalism), for no one is made righteous by good works.
   b. The Gospel is good news because it delivers man from the judgment of God's law.

III. Justification is God's way of declaring a person righteous.
   a. *Simul iustus et peccator*: We are justified sinners.
   b. Is this a legal fiction?
   c. Justification is *by* faith alone.
   d. The instrumental cause of justification, according to the Roman Catholic church, is baptism.
   e. According to Reformed theology, the instrument is faith.
   f. Mortal sin destroys justification in the Roman system, but through penance and the sacraments, it can be restored. So Rome has two causes of justification: baptism and penance.

g. The struggle of the sixteenth century came down to the difference between infusion and imputation.
h. The righteousness of Christ for us, not in us, is the key to our justification.
i. Christ was being punished for our sins, not His, when He was on the cross. Imputation is the legal transfer of our guilt to Christ and then the transfer of Christ's righteousness to us.

STUDY QUESTIONS

1. What is the instrumental cause of justification, according to Reformed theology?
   a. Faith
   b. Penance
   c. Baptism
   d. Works

2. The concept of being simultaneously "justified and a sinner" is a legal fiction.
   a. True
   b. False

3. Justification is an act of God whereby He declares unjust sinners to be just after He has ________________.
   a. Offered to them the righteousness of Christ
   b. Required of them the righteousness of Christ
   c. Infused into them the righteousness of Christ
   d. Imputed to them the righteousness of Christ

4. How many instrumental causes of justification are there, according to Rome?
   a. One
   b. Two
   c. Three
   d. Four

5. In Rome's view, how can justification be lost?
   a. By committing a venial sin
   b. By committing a mortal sin
   c. By committing a heinous sin
   d. By committing a gross sin

6. What phrase best captures the concept of our sin's being counted to Christ and His righteousness' being counted to us?
   a. A double transfer
   b. A forensic declaration
   c. A synthetic statement
   d. A legal fiction

DISCUSSION QUESTIONS

1. What was the formal cause of the Reformation?

2. What was the material cause of the Reformation?

3. What does the term *justification* mean?

4. What is the instrumental cause of justification according to Protestants? According to Roman Catholics?

42

Saving Faith

INTRODUCTION

What is saving faith? This question received a deserved amount of attention at the time of the Reformation, and it should receive just as much attention from us today. In this lesson, Dr. Sproul examines the three ingredients of saving faith asserted by the Reformers.

MESSAGE OVERVIEW

I. Do Catholics believe that we are saved by works?
   a. No. They call faith the foundation of justification. But it is not sufficient to justify us. There also must be works, at least the works of penance.
   b. Rome believes we need grace plus merit.

II. What is saving faith?
   a. Luther was accused of teaching a cheap faith, antinomianism, or the freedom to live as you please as long as you intellectually affirm the right things.
   b. If a man says that he has faith but not works, can that faith save him?
   c. *Fides viva*, or "a living faith," is what we must have for salvation. We are saved by faith alone, but not by a faith that is alone.
   d. Our works do not form any grounds for our justification.

III. What are the elements of saving faith?
   a. *Notitia*, or knowledge, refers to the content of our faith.
   b. *Assensus* refers to our emotional readiness to affirm the truth.
   c. *Fiducia*, or trust, refers to our faith in God.

IV. What is conversion and what are the other benefits of saving faith?
   a. Conversion is synergistic—we perform repentance as a part of it.
   b. *Metanoia* means "a changing of the mind."

c. Adoption is another benefit of saving faith.
d. The fruits of justification mentioned in Romans 5 are peace with God and access to Him.

STUDY QUESTIONS

1. Which of the following is the Reformed view of the relationship between faith, works, and justification?
   a. Works - faith = justification
   b. Faith + works = justification
   c. Faith = justification + works
   d. Faith = justification - works

2. The Latin phrase *fides viva* means "a living faith."
   a. True
   b. False

3. Which of the following is not an element of saving faith?
   a. *Assensus*
   b. *Metanoia*
   c. *Fiducia*
   d. *Notitia*

4. What kind of work of God is conversion (i.e., faith and repentance)?
   a. Synergistic
   b. Monergistic
   c. Cooperative
   d. Cumulative

5. What is the first fruit of our justification?
   a. Peace with God
   b. Fellowship with God
   c. Love for God
   d. Obedience towards God

6. What immediately comes after our justification?
   a. Sanctification
   b. Empowerment
   c. Glorification
   d. Adoption

DISCUSSION QUESTIONS

1. Does Roman Catholic theology teach that we are justified by works? Explain.
2. What did Luther mean by the Latin phrase *fides viva*?
3. Name and define the three elements of Christian faith?
4. What is the meaning of repentance?

43

Adoption and Union with Christ

INTRODUCTION

To be part of the family of God is a gift. It is not something that believers earn, nor is it something that they have by the sheer virtue of being human. In this lesson, Dr. Sproul explains the special privilege of being a child of God through adoption and union with Christ.

MESSAGE OVERVIEW

I. The apostle John calls us "children of God." This is no small thing.
   a. In our culture, we take for granted that all people are children of God. Nineteenth century liberal theology has polluted our culture at this point.
   b. Von Harnack's *What is Christianity?* said that the universal fatherhood of God and the universal brotherhood of man were the essence of Christianity.
   c. The fatherhood of God is a radical concept. In the first century, it was an astonishing idea that anyone could be related to God.
   d. J. Jeremias studied the idea of the fatherhood of God in Judaism. "Father" was not among the titles that people called God.
   e. Jesus, however, went on to call God "Father" frequently. Judaism did not refer to God as "Father" until the tenth century A.D.

II. Jesus extended the privilege of calling God "Father" to His disciples.
   a. In the Lord's Prayer, Jesus told His disciples to pray to "our" Father.
   b. This immediately passed on the truth of God's Fatherhood to His people.
   c. We obscure the idea of sonship to God when we say things like, "If the Holy Spirit lives inside you, you are as much a son of God as Jesus is." This fails to protect the unique nature of Jesus' Sonship.

III. The unique nature of Jesus' Sonship is shown in John 1, especially around verse 10.
   a. "As many as received Him, He gave the power [or authority] to be called the children of God." So sonship is a gift.
   b. Romans 8:12 says that we are sons of God who are led by the Spirit of God, the Spirit of adoption.
   c. God brings us into His family when we are regenerated. We are a part of the family of God. The elect are all God's adopted children.

IV. The mystical union of the believer with Christ is a mystery. It transcends our natural experience.
   a. The Greek words *en* (in) and *eis* (into) describe the nature of our union with Christ. Once we have gone *into* Christ, then we are *in* Christ.
   b. If I am in Christ, if He is in me and I am in Him, what does that say about my relationships with others in the church? This union extends beyond "me and Jesus," creating the bond of unity we experience with true believers.

STUDY QUESTIONS

1. What did Adolf von Harnack erroneously teach concerning all people?
   a. We are all God's creatures.
   b. We are all God's manifestations.
   c. We are all God's image-bearers.
   d. We are all God's children.

2. To whom did the Lord's Prayer extended the privilege of calling God "Father"?
   a. All disciples
   b. All creation
   c. All people
   d. All angels

3. Those who have the Holy Spirit within them are as much sons of God in every way as Jesus is the Son of God.
   a. True
   b. False

4. What was the Greek word that Dr. Sproul used to describe our mystical union with Christ?
   a. *Eis* (into)
   b. *En* (in)
   c. *Se* (in)
   d. *Entos* (within)

5. When was the first reference in print that mentioned a Jewish person directly addressing God as Father in prayer?
   a. The tenth century AD
   b. The twelfth century BC
   c. The third century AD
   d. The second century BC

6. What reality of Christ is central to the New Testament?
   a. His deity
   b. His human nature
   c. His eternal life
   d. His sonship

DISCUSSION QUESTIONS

1. What is the essence of Christianity, according to Adolf Von Harnack?

2. Why was Jesus' use of the title "Father" shocking to first century Jews?

3. What biblical passages describe the unique Sonship of Christ?

4. How does our union with Christ affect our view of the communion of saints?

44

Sanctification

INTRODUCTION

When someone has been justified by faith in Christ, the transformative work of sanctification begins. In this lesson, Dr. Sproul discusses the path of sanctification in the Christian life and the impact that it has for believers' growth in grace.

MESSAGE OVERVIEW

I. Sanctification is partial, but real.
   a. When Dr. Sproul first became a Christian, he would listen to R.J. Lamont as he drove. "What's on your partially sanctified mind?"
   b. Justification is not partial. It is immediate.
   c. It is bad news that our sanctification is partial, but it is real. By it the people of God are actually made holy. Sanctification begins immediately after regeneration.
   d. The fruit of our sanctification is inevitable and immediate. People cannot be converted to Christ and never bring forth fruits. There are no "carnal" Christians.
   e. We are not justified by the profession of faith, but the possession of faith.

II. Our growth in sanctification is not a straight line. It has peaks and valleys. Sometimes we may enter very dark valleys. Maturity means the peaks and valleys are smoothed out a bit.
   a. Some in the church teach perfectionism, an instantaneous infusion of God's sanctifying grace.
   b. Others believe in a "leap" corresponding to belief in certain doctrines or experiences. The error here is that one doctrine or experience cannot cause, mechanistically, a victorious Christian life.
   c. It is a rare thing for a Christian to see immediate victory over some sin. Nothing happens fast. There are no three easy steps to growth.

   d. In Philippians 2:12–13, Paul says we should work out our own salvation, but that God is working with us even more so.
   e. Note that "fear and trembling" is a real part of the work of sanctification.
   f. Sanctification is a cooperative process. It is synergistic, not monergistic. We are active at some points and passive at others.

III. The errors of activism and quietism are evident in the theology of sanctification today.
   a. Being active without embracing activism is as simple as not being a legalist. Self-righteousness is the danger here, and activism teaches a self-reliance that is deadly.
   b. Quietism says that we should "Let go and let God." There are times to be passive and depend upon God, no doubt. But the teaching that we can offer nothing to the work of sanctification is deadly.
   c. Antinomianism and legalism are also distortions of the doctrine of sanctification. The legalist legislates where God has given us freedom. The antinomian gives freedom where God has given real direction. But we may not create new laws and we may not ignore the ones He plainly has given.
   d. Avoiding these errors will go far to aid our sanctification.

STUDY QUESTIONS

1. In this life, what is sanctification?
   a. Futile
   b. Complete
   c. Partial
   d. Effortless

2. Because sinless perfection is impossible, it is possible to be a "carnal Christian."
   a. True
   b. False

3. What is the error of thinking that says we can contribute nothing to our sanctification?
   a. Quietism
   b. Activism
   c. Antinomianism
   d. Perfectionism

4. While the legalist gives commands where God gives freedom, what does the antinomian give where God gives direction?
   a. Commands
   b. Freedom
   c. Scripture
   d. Tradition

5. What should be the response of the Christian to the law of God?
   a. To love it
   b. To flee from it
   c. To add to it
   d. To rewrite it

6. What heresy teaches that Christians can accomplish their sanctification by themselves?
   a. Quietism
   b. Legalism
   c. Activism
   d. Antinomianism

DISCUSSION QUESTIONS

1. What is perfectionism? Is this doctrine dangerous? Why or why not?

2. What is quietism?

3. What is activism?

4. What is the difference between antinomianism and legalism? Why are both of these errors harmful to the body of Christ?

45

Perseverance of the Saints

INTRODUCTION

The New Testament gives us confidence that God is going to preserve His own and bring His work of redemption to completion. In this lesson, Dr. Sproul addresses the question of whether Christians have the ability to lose their salvation.

MESSAGE OVERVIEW

I. What is "tubing it"?
   a. People get involved with religious things, but then they drop out, stop coming to church, and repudiate Christ.
   b. Those who are truly converted do not fall away. But as we make Christianity more appealing to the unconverted, they often "accept" Jesus but do not deal with their sin and repent.
   c. The parable of the sower helps us understand the background to spurious conversions.

II. The Roman Catholic doctrine of salvation teaches that we can lose our salvation through mortal sin.
   a. Mortal sin makes it necessary for us to have a new penance, a new justification.
   b. Semi-Pelagians also believe we can lose our salvation, a belief springing from their free-will theology.
   c. Election and perseverance go together. There is no question that perseverance flows logically from election. The question is whether perseverance flows from the Bible.

III. What is the biblical evidence for the perseverance of the saints?
   a. Philippians teaches a clear doctrine of perseverance. "He who began a good work in you will be faithful to complete it." This is without doubt. But there

are problematic passages that cause some to doubt the force of passages like these.

b. Hebrews 6:1–6 is such a passage. Does this go against the teaching of Paul to the people of Philippi?
c. Some suggest that the author of Hebrews is not describing regenerate people, only church members. But read Hebrews 6:4–6 and see whether all these descriptions would allow for a such a reading. The key point is "brought back to repentance." Could unbelievers ever be said to repent in the first place? No.
d. Does this not lead to a denial of perseverance? No. But it does seem that the writer is speaking of believers.
e. The answer to this problem is found by discovering the audience to which this was written. The author seems to be writing to people in danger of the Judaizing heresy.
f. If that is true, the writer could be using the *ad hominem* argument, taking his opponent's presuppositions and making an argument with them, against the opponent. See Hebrews 6:9, which seems to say he has been speaking off-handedly, not teaching in a straightforward way.
g. This seems to be the answer: the writer is speaking using the Judaizers' own logic against them. This section then would not be a repudiation of the teaching from Philippians.

IV. The preservation of the saints is accomplished by God. He has promised not to rest until we are found perfect.

STUDY QUESTIONS

1. No one who receives the gospel can lose his salvation.
   a. True
   b. False

2. In the Roman Catholic Church, what causes one to lose his justification, making penance necessary?
   a. Venial sins
   b. Lesser sins
   c. Any sins
   d. Mortal sins

3. What heresy is the author of Hebrews likely addressing in his letter?
   a. The Arian heresy
   b. The Gnostic heresy
   c. The Judaizing heresy
   d. The Nestorian heresy

4. Who is the author of Hebrews speaking of when he says that there are people who fall away and do not experience restoration (Heb. 6:4–6)?
   a. A regenerate person
   b. An unregenerate person
   c. A reconciled person
   d. An unreconciled person

5. Even though perseverance is based on the promises of God, what may a true believer still experience?
   a. Habitual sin
   b. A serious fall
   c. Seasons of doubt
   d. Hopelessness

6. What term could be used in place of the word *perseverance*?
   a. Exultation
   b. Striving
   c. Endurance
   d. Preservation

DISCUSSION QUESTIONS

1. What is the difference between a mortal sin and a venial sin in Roman Catholic theology?

2. What are some of the biblical passages that teach the perseverance of the saints?

3. Does Hebrews 6 undermine the doctrine of the perseverance of the saints? Explain.

4. Why does the doctrine of election necessitate the doctrine of perseverance?

46

Biblical Images of the Church

INTRODUCTION

Ecclesiology is the subdivision of systematic theology that has to do with the nature, function, and mission of the church. In this lesson, Dr. Sproul defines the true meaning of the church as the people of God from the aspects of the visible and invisible church.

MESSAGE OVERVIEW

I. The church is described in the Bible with many titles and metaphors.
    a. The background of the English word *church* is found by observing the various names for "church" around the world. They are commonly derived from the Greek *kuriache,* or those who are possessed by the *kurios,* or Lord.
    b. *Ekklesia* is another Greek word that we translate "church." This Greek word is based on the verb *kaleo,* or "to call."
    c. Augustine described the church as a *corpus per mixtum*, a mixed body. Wheat and tares exist together in the visible church. In our vernacular, it is a "mixed bag."
        i. The invisible church
        ii. The visible church
        iii. Not two separate spheres but distinct.
        iv. The true people of God are largely a part of the visible church

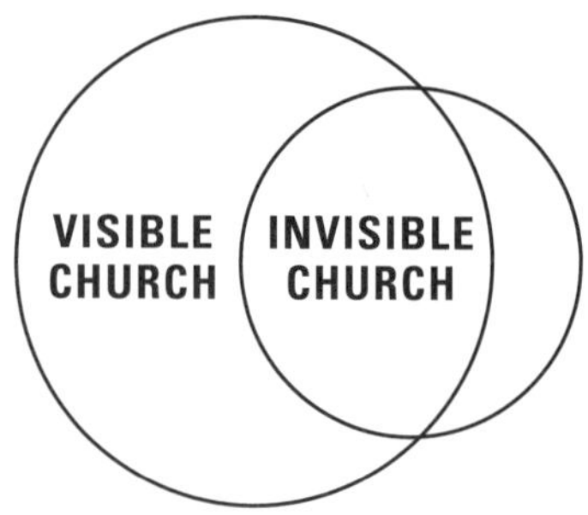

STUDY QUESTIONS

1. What does the Greek word *kuriache* mean?
    a. Those who are chosen by God
    b. Those who belong to the Lord
    c. Those who are part of the elect
    d. Those who are loved by God

2. The Greek word *kaleō* is the root for which of the following English words?
   a. Church
   b. Priesthood
   c. Cathedral
   d. Ecclesiastical

3. What reality is indicated by the Latin phrase *corpus per mixtum*?
   a. The church is a mixed body.
   b. The church is visible and invisible.
   c. The church is made up of believers only.
   d. The church is made up of believers and their children.

4. Where is the invisible church found?
   a. In heaven
   b. In your local church
   c. In the visible church
   d. In a church's membership roles

5. Which sin is cause for excommunication?
   a. Adultery
   b. Apostasy
   c. Heresy
   d. Impenitence

6. It is possible for a true believer to be found within a Mormon or Roman Catholic church.
   a. True
   b. False

DISCUSSION QUESTIONS

1. What is the background of the English word *church*?

2. What is the basic meaning of the Greek word *ekklesia*?

3. What is the difference between the invisible church and the visible church?

4. What is the significance of Augustine's description of the church as a *corpus per mixtum*?

47

The Church: One and Holy

INTRODUCTION

The qualities of the church are reflected in the New Testament imagery of the church as one body and a building with one sure foundation. In this lesson, Dr. Sproul explains the unity and diversity within the one church.

MESSAGE OVERVIEW

I. There are other metaphors used to describe the church.
   a. The church is described as a body, with Jesus Christ as the head.
   b. The church is also called the *Laos Theou,* or the "People of God."
   c. The church is described as a building, built on the foundation of the apostles and prophets, with Christ as the chief cornerstone. The rest of the church is made up of the individual stones.

II. What are the chief characteristics of the church?
   a. In the fourth century, the church was defined as one, holy, catholic, and apostolic in its character.
   b. These terms are rarely used in Protestantism, but they remain an excellent description of the true church.

III. What does it mean that we are "one"?
   a. The church is a community of saints, or *communio sanctorum.*
   b. The visible church always will be fragmented. The invisible church is necessarily one.
   c. Why should we split? Certainly not over minor matters. The error of schismatic behavior is as bad as remaining linked to a corrupt body.

IV. What does it mean that the church is holy"?
   a. No institution has been so gifted as the church of God. When we fail to obey the mission God has given us, relatively speaking, we are more blameworthy.
   b. So how can we say the church is holy? We appear to be very unholy.
   c. "Holy" means "set apart." The church is holy in the sense that it has a sacred mission. And God has promised that the church will not fail in her mission. The gates of hell will not prevail against her.
   d. The church is subject to the concentrated ministry of the Holy Spirit.
   e. The church is where the saints (holy ones) are gathered, so this makes the church a holy institution as well.

STUDY QUESTIONS

1. In Paul's analogy of a building, what is the foundation of the church?
   a. Christ the cornerstone
   b. The people of god
   c. The Apostles and prophets
   d. Love and unity among believers

2. What is one of the major motivations for unity in the church?
   a. Scandals in the church
   b. The proliferation of denominations
   c. Hypocrisy in the church
   d. Heresy

3. Breaking fellowship with part of the visible church also destroys the unity of the invisible church.
   a. True
   b. False

4. What does *communio sanctorum* mean?
   a. Community of believers
   b. Community of Christians
   c. Community of saints
   d. Sacred community

5. According to Scripture, what does it mean to be holy?
   a. To be set apart
   b. To be perfect
   c. To be majestic
   d. To be beyond corruption

6. Which of the following makes the church holy?
   a. The Holy Spirit
   b. Good works
   c. Apostolic succession
   d. The Word of God

DISCUSSION QUESTIONS

1. What are some of the biblical metaphors used to describe the church? What aspects of the church do each of these metaphors communicate?

2. What do we mean when we say we believe the church is "one"?

3. Why is schism such a serious sin?

4. What do we mean when we say we believe the church is "holy"?

48

The Church: Catholic and Apostolic

INTRODUCTION

The characteristics of the church as catholic and Apostolic are often misunderstood by Protestants today. In this lesson, Dr. Sproul defines these terms according to the universal nature and Apostolic foundation of the church.

MESSAGE OVERVIEW

I. One day, I was on a train to Romania . . .

II. The third characteristic of the church is that it is "catholic," or universal.
   a. The Apostles' Creed says that we believe in the "catholic" church. But this is not referring to the Roman institution.
   b. The fellowship of the church goes beyond regional boundaries.

III. The final characteristic of the church is that it is apostolic.
   a. In the first century, the primary authority in the church was vested in the apostles. An *apostolos* is one who is sent from a *kurios* to represent him.
   b. There is a significant difference between the disciples (learners) of Christ and His apostles.
   c. Those who rejected the apostles rejected Jesus. Groups such as the Gnostics disputed the authority of the apostles, but tried to keep an allegiance to Jesus and other biblical characters.
   d. Apostolic authority is challenged today, especially by higher critics and feminist theologians.
   e. Those who attack the foundations of the church may appear to continue in the church, but when the foundation is destroyed, the building is unlivable.
   f. The abandonment of apostolic authority is at the heart of the demise of the visible church in Europe.

g. During the Reformation, as today, it was debated as to who was *the* true church. The question is stated more accurately, "What is *a* true church?" "What are its marks?"
    i. Proper preaching of the Gospel
    ii. Proper administration of the sacraments
    iii. Proper discipline and government of God's people

STUDY QUESTIONS

1. The term *catholic* in the Apostles' Creed refers to the Roman Catholic Church.
    a. True
    b. False

2. What is an Apostle?
    a. A student of Christ's teachings
    b. A follower of Christ
    c. One of the twelve disciples
    d. A disciple endowed with Christ's authority

3. What does *apostolos* mean?
    a. One who is set apart
    b. One who is sent
    c. One who speaks in tongues
    d. One who is spiritually elite

4. What is Apostolic authority?
    a. The foundation of the church
    b. Authority of the saints
    c. Apostolic rank
    d. Authority of Paul

5. What is the first mark of a true church?
    a. The sacrament of baptism
    b. The preaching of the gospel
    c. The sacrament of the Lord's Supper
    d. The practice of church discipline

6. What does church discipline require?
    a. Self-government
    b. Order of worship
    c. Private confession
    d. Church government

DISCUSSION QUESTIONS

1. Explain what we mean when we confess our belief that the church is "catholic."
2. What do mean when we say that we believe the church is "apostolic"?
3. What is the difference between an apostle and a disciple?
4. During the Reformation, what were said to be the "marks" of a true church?

49

Worship in the Church

INTRODUCTION

Worship is the central purpose of the church and therefore should not be neglected or overlooked. In this lesson, Dr. Sproul takes a look at the question, What is true worship?

MESSAGE OVERVIEW

I. Revelation 5 is one of the most powerful passages of worship in the Bible.
  a. Every Christian should be able to relate to this kind of heavenly worship.
  b. We were created to worship God. Once we are regenerate, we have a capacity and a hunger to express the worth and value of God.
  c. One of the key functions of God's church is to express worship.

II. Worship is the vocation of the church. But what is worship?
  a. Worship is a measure of worth, value or honor. Worship honors God as God.
  b. Romans 1 teaches that, in our fallen state, our basic sin is refusal to worship God.
  c. In the Old Testament, worship was seen primarily as an offering or a sacrifice. Some sacrifices were done simply to honor God. Music and praise were seen as a kind of sacrifice in that system, and it is not error to give this kind of sacrifice today (Rom. 12:1–2).
  d. Adoration is another kind of worship that is characterized by expressions of intense love from our inmost being. This is a spiritual expression of love that defies precise definition.

III. What does it mean to worship God in "spirit and in truth"?
  a. John 4 is where Jesus meets the Samaritan woman and tells her how to worship God. But what does it mean?

b. The second part is not too difficult. We are not to worship God falsely—neither through idolatry nor hypocrisy.
c. The first part is more difficult. It probably refers to "soulful" worship, worship that flows from the heart, from the very depths of our being.
d. During the Reformation, the priority was proper worship of God. All the Reformers were concerned with worshiping God in truth, that is, purifying their churches from idolatry.
e. The patterns of worship were dictated in Old Testament times. One principle we can learn from this was that the entire person should be involved in worship: the mind and the five senses. The heart? The will? The spirit?

STUDY QUESTIONS

1. As creatures made in the image of God, what did God create us for?
   a. Dominion
   b. Worship
   c. Fellowship
   d. Glory

2. To worship God is to attribute worth or value to God.
   a. True
   b. False

3. If we are not worshiping God, what are we worshiping?
   a. Creator
   b. Celebrities
   c. Creatures
   d. Ourselves

4. What word used in connection with worship is connected to the Old Testament sin offering?
   a. Exaltation
   b. Praise
   c. Sacrifice
   d. Adoration

5. What type of love is associated with adoration?
   a. Passionate love
   b. Worshipful love
   c. Romantic love
   d. Affectionate love

6. What kind of worship is pleasing to God?
    a. False worship
    b. Hypocritical worship
    c. Soulful worship
    d. Corporate worship

DISCUSSION QUESTIONS

1. Is worship a matter of taste or obedience?

2. Why is worship so significant in the life of the church?

3. What changes in worship were due to the inauguration of the new covenant at Christ's first coming?

4. What does it mean to worship God "in spirit and in truth"?

50

The Sacraments of the Church

INTRODUCTION

The sacraments of baptism and the Lord's Supper have caused considerable controversy within the church, but for good reason. In this lesson, Dr. Sproul explains the importance and seriousness of the sacraments as gifts of Christ to the church.

MESSAGE OVERVIEW

I. It is the privilege of an ordained minister to administer the sacraments.
   a. As important as it is, sacramentology is a hotly debated issue, with many controversies surrounding it.
   b. One reason we use the word *sacraments* is that these actions are sacred.
   c. This explains the seriousness of the debate.

II. The number of the sacraments of the church is one of the debated issues.
   a. The Roman Catholic Church has seven sacraments, all of which are said to infuse grace into the soul.
   b. The first sacrament administered is baptism. It pours the grace of justification into the soul. This grace is *ex opere operato*, which means "through the working of the works."
   c. The sacrament does not work automatically, but it can be hindered by the recipient.
   d. Even if a Catholic loses his justification, he is not rebaptized.
   e. At confirmation, the second sacrament, new grace is given to the child to prepare him for this new phase of his life.
   f. Penance is the third sacrament. It is the "second plank" of justification. Grace is infused and, if justification is lost, it can be regained via penance.
   g. Matrimony is the fourth sacrament and, as before, gives grace to those about to be married.

h. Holy orders is the fifth sacrament. It is given to those in ministry to enable them to dispense grace and offer the prayer of consecration, which changes the bread and wine into the body and blood of Christ.
i. The sixth sacrament is extreme unction. It originally was not called "last rites," but was based on James 5, an anointing for healing.
j. The sacrament we have left out is the eucharist. The Lord's Supper dispenses grace to the recipient. It will be discussed in full in a subsequent lecture.

III. The Protestants reduced the seven sacraments to two.
a. Luther wrote *The Babylonian Captivity of the Church* against the sacerdotalism of the Roman institution. Sacramental salvation was attacked in this book and justification by faith alone was exalted.
b. The Reformers said that the sacraments must have been directly instituted by Christ. This limited the number to two. Other activities, such as ordination, could be ordinances, but not sacraments.
c. The Reformers also said that the sacraments functioned *ex opera operantis,* meaning that the benefits are received by faith.
d. Sacraments are signs and seals. They are the Word dramatized. They represent God's guarantee that we will receive the benefits of salvation.

STUDY QUESTIONS

1. What are baptism and the Lord's Supper called?
   a. Institutions
   b. Sacraments
   c. Gifts of grace
   d. Confirmation

2. How many sacraments are there in the Roman Catholic Church?
   a. Seven
   b. Six
   c. Five
   d. Four

3. During the Reformation, the debate over which sacrament was the underlying issue of justification?
   a. Baptism
   b. Penance
   c. Eucharist
   d. Confirmation

4. What does *ex opere operato* mean?
    a. Through the workings of grace
    b. Through the workings of the works
    c. Through the automatic works
    d. Through the power of works

5. According to Rome, which sacrament marks the soul?
    a. Eucharist
    b. Confirmation
    c. Baptism
    d. Reconciliation

6. In his book *The Babylonian Captivity of the Church*, what did Luther lash out against in the Roman Catholic system?
    a. Popes
    b. Priesthood
    c. Indulgences
    d. Sacerdotalism

DISCUSSION QUESTIONS

1. What is the meaning of the term *sacrament*?

2. What are the seven sacraments of Roman Catholicism?

3. What two sacraments do Protestants recognize?

4. What reasons do Protestants give for recognizing only two sacraments?

51

Baptism

INTRODUCTION

Baptism is a significant moment in every Christian's life because it is an sacrament instituted by Christ as a sign and seal of God's promises. In this lesson, Dr. Sproul answers important questions surrounding the meaning, origin, and significance of baptism.

MESSAGE OVERVIEW

I. The sacrament of baptism is practiced in a variety of ways.
   a. We baptize adults and children, and we do so for different reasons.
   b. Are you baptized? So what?
   c. The baptism of John the Baptist is not the model for baptism today. It was directed specifically to the Jews, who were technically in Old Testament times. It should not be used as a pattern for today.
   d. There was a Jewish practice known as proselyte baptism, one performed on Gentiles. John the Baptist proclaimed the need for Jews to be baptized in a similar manner.

II. When Jesus instituted the new covenant, He gave new signs to represent it.
   a. Remember that God gave a sign to Noah to represent the covenant God made with him.
   b. God gave a sign for the old covenant as well: circumcision.
   c. Paul asked, "What advantage is it to be a Jew?" The question was rhetorical—he was saying that the things that made them Jewish (such as the bearing of covenant signs) were not insignificant.
   d. The cutting of circumcision represented not only the blessings of the covenant, but the cursings as well. On this basis, Paul was completely opposed to the Judaizing movement (see Galatians).

e. There is significant continuity between the old covenant and the new. But not identity. They are not separate, but they are distinct.
f. The reality of our union with Christ is made clearer by our baptism. God has made promises to us, and baptism reminds us of those promises.
g. In Colossians 2:8–12, Paul discusses exactly what the rite of baptism signifies for us.
h. If I were the only person in the world God had ordained to save, then Jesus would have had to die on the cross for my sins.
i. There is a continual deepening of our identification with Christ throughout the Christian life. Baptism symbolizes our participation with Christ.

III. Who qualifies for baptism?
  a. Just as the Old Testament signs were given to believers and their children, the New Testament signs likewise were given. This command was nowhere recanted or altered.
  b. The Old Testament sign also symbolized faith in God—there is no change at this point in the New Testament.
  c. The validity of baptism depends not on the recipient or the baptizer, but on God.

STUDY QUESTIONS

1. New Testament baptism is the same thing as the baptism of John the Baptist.
   a. True
   b. False

2. Which practice was a purification right for gentiles in the covenant community?
   a. Profession of faith
   b. Circumcision
   c. Proselyte baptism
   d. Sin offering

3. What was the sign and seal of the old covenant?
   a. Animal sacrifice
   b. Circumcision
   c. Baptism
   d. Passover

4. Who fulfilled the negative sanctions of circumcision?
   a. Abraham
   b. Adam
   c. Christ
   d. Moses

5. What do we possess in baptism?
    a. Salvation
    b. God's promises
    c. Regeneration
    d. Confirmation

6. How do we participate with Christ in His suffering?
    a. Through baptism
    b. Through faith
    c. Through circumcision
    d. Through atonement

DISCUSSION QUESTIONS

1. What are the different modes of baptism? What are the doctrines or concepts that surround each one?

2. What is the key word to describe baptism in the Bible and in this lecture?

3. Who is qualified for baptism? Is there anyone to whom baptism should be refused?

52

The Lord's Supper

INTRODUCTION

Throughout church history, the sacrament of the Lord's Supper has been a central concern of the church. In this lesson, Dr. Sproul introduces and distinguishes between the Roman Catholic, Lutheran, and Reformed views of the Lord's Supper.

MESSAGE OVERVIEW

I. The New Testament makes the Lord's Supper a central part of the corporate worship of the church.
   a. The book of Acts records this event (Acts 2).
   b. The Passover meal Jesus shared with His disciples emphasizes the importance of this sacrament.
   c. Jesus changes the classical wording of the Passover rite when He makes reference to the bread being His body and the wine His blood.
   d. This announcement of the new covenant marks an important point in redemptive history: the beginning of the new covenant and the end of the old. Christ's death becomes central to the Christian faith from this point on.

II. But theological controversy has come from this event in the Upper Room. A major point of division for Christians around the world is the exact nature of the Lord's Supper, both its essence and form.
   a. The Protestant Reformation marked a separation from the Catholic errors concerning the sacraments, but among themselves, the Protestants could not agree on the mode or manner of the presence of Christ in the sacraments.
   b. Luther retreated to the words of institution: *Hoc est corpus meum*—"This is My body."
   c. Priests did the Mass in Latin, which was unknown to the people. They were ridiculed by the common man, who said things like, "Look at the priest and all his hocus pocus!" This portion of the Mass is where that phrase originates.

III. The major views of the Lord's Supper are claimed by the Roman Catholics, the Lutherans, the Anabaptists, and the Calvinists.
  a. The Roman Catholic view is that the bread and wine literally become the body and blood of Jesus. The response of the people is, "Hey, it still looks like bread and wine, and not only that, it tastes the same!"
  b. The doctrine of transubstantiation was developed to answer these objections. The philosopher Aristotle said that all objects are made up of substance and accidens. The raw matter and the appearance to the senses of a given object were separated in his system.
  c. So in the miracle of the Mass, the substance (inner core, essence) of the bread and wine change. The accidens, or appearance, does not. This was a double miracle—not only did the substance change, but the accidens did not follow that change. Supernaturally, the accidens is sustained even though the substance changes.
  d. Objection: Luther said this is more miraculous than necessary. Jesus can be physically present without the bread and wine being changed. Jesus is added to the bread and wine; thus we call this view consubstantiation. The "con" means "with."
  e. Calvin objected to all of these views; he was concerned that a physical body (which Jesus has) can be in only one place at a time, and Jesus says His is in heaven. Thus, Jesus' body (which is clearly said to be present in some way by Rome and Luther) can't be present in the sacraments in any form. But the divine nature of Jesus can be everywhere at once. The divine nature of Christ is therefore present at the Lord's Supper. He is really there, but spiritually, not physically.
  f. The Anabaptists view the Lord's Supper merely as a memorial. There is no miracle and no grace is communicated; we only perform a holy duty as instructed by our Lord (*point f not covered in the lecture, but included for completion*).

IV. The time factors of the past, present, and future relate to the Lord's Supper.
  a. The Lord's Supper focuses us on the past, as the Anabaptists emphasize.
  b. It also focuses us on the present meeting we have with Jesus as we partake of the bread and wine, as taught by the other three positions in some way.
  c. It also focuses us on our future, on the time when we will sit with Jesus and all the saints and happily partake of His holy food in heaven.

STUDY QUESTIONS

1. When did the New Testament begin?
   a. With John the Baptist
   b. With the incarnation
   c. With the Lord's Supper
   d. With Christ's ministry

2. Which Old Testament practice did Jesus redefine in the upper room?
   a. Passover
   b. Circumcision
   c. Baptism
   d. Sacrifice

3. What is the Roman Catholic view of the Lord's Supper?
   a. Transubstantiation
   b. Consubstantiation
   c. Transignification
   d. Suprasubstantiation

4. According to Aristotle, what is another word for the *essence* of an object?
   a. Form
   b. Matter
   c. Substance
   d. Accidents

5. What does the Latin prefix *con* mean?
   a. Contra
   b. With
   c. In
   d. Through

6. What was the main issue the Reformers had with the Lord's Supper?
   a. The substance and accidents of the elements
   b. The believability of Christ's presence
   c. The mode and manner of Christ's presence
   d. The past, present, and future of the Lord's Supper

DISCUSSION QUESTIONS

1. What important point of redemptive history does the Lord's Supper celebrate?

2. What are the various views in Protestantism concerning the Lord's Supper? How do they agree? How do they differ?

3. What is the view of your church? How can your church better perform the Lord's Supper?

53

Death and the Intermediate State

INTRODUCTION

Eschatology is the study of the last days and our future hope of redemption. As such, it deals with the most perplexing problems of life: death. In this lesson, Dr. Sproul discusses the last enemy and helps us understand what happens to God's people when they die.

MESSAGE OVERVIEW

I. This section of our study deals with eschatology. This word is derived from the Greek word *eschaton*, meaning "last." The beginning of this study is a frank look at death.
   a. Death is the last enemy to be subdued by Christ.
   b. "If a man dies, will he live again?"
   c. What does death mean to the Christian?

II. Paul's letter to the Romans explains the origin and current nature of death.
   a. Romans 5:14 asks, "Was there sin prior to Moses' law?" The answer is "Yes," because death existed, and without law there is no sin. Without sin there can be no death.
   b. Death is not a part of the natural order of things. It is a part of the fallen order of things.
   c. When God told Adam and Eve that when they sinned they would die, He was speaking spiritually. But the curse had a physical component as well: They were rendered under the power of death from that time on. It was an act of mercy that they were allowed to live so long after their sin. All of us are on "death row" because of sin.
   d. From a Christian perspective, death is not the punishment for sin. Jesus Christ has paid that penalty. In light of the Cross, death is a moment of transition. Its significance has changed.

III. Paul's message to us from Philippians is that death has an aspect of victory and blessing, as well as defeat.
   a. In 1:19ff, Paul says that he is torn between praying to stay on earth or dying and being with Christ. Our faith staggers at this statement of Paul's faith in the immediate care for His soul by Jesus.
   b. Many Christians are unafraid of death. But the process we may have to go through to die is very fearsome. Dying can be terribly painful, and God does not promise to spare us from suffering.
   c. Paul's passionate faith and fearless determination come through in this passage. Paul saw dying for Christ as a gain. Perhaps it would be a loss for his beloved left on this earth, but it would be a gain for him.
   d. Life and death were seen by Paul as the good and the far better.

IV. What happens to us when we die?
   a. "I believe in the resurrection of the body." This refers to our belief that, though we die, God will raise us from the grave.
   b. First Corinthians 15 teaches that, just as Christ was raised, we will be raised from the dead. What will we look like? Paul does not know. But we will be able to recognize each other.
   c. We will have glorified bodies. But between the time of our deaths and our resurrections, our souls reside in heaven. We will be souls without bodies, souls that are active and aware. There is an unbroken continuity of personal existence. There is no soul sleep.
   d. Even though we are in changing bodies and changing circumstances, our minds remain unchanged. Our personalities remain unchanged, by and large. Just because our souls are in a time of transition does not mean they must sleep.

STUDY QUESTIONS

1. What is eschatology the study of?
   a. The last things
   b. The antichrist
   c. The rapture
   d. The afterlife

2. What is the Christian view of death?
   a. It is the end of life.
   b. It is a natural part of life.
   c. It is punishment for sin.
   d. It represents spiritual death.

3. If the penalty for sin is death, why did Adam and Eve not die when they ate the forbidden fruit?
   a. God lied.
   b. God was gracious.
   c. God only meant a spiritual death.
   d. It was an empty threat.

4. What is the significance of death in the Christian's life?
   a. It is a state of transition.
   b. It is part of human suffering.
   c. It is a taste of hell.
   d. It is part of the curse.

5. For Paul, to live was Christ, and to die was ______.
   a. Loss
   b. Gain
   c. Pain
   d. Good

6. According to which view is there a period of unconscious "suspended animation" of the soul between death and the final resurrection?
   a. Annihilationism
   b. Conditionalism
   c. Soul sleep
   d. Purgatory

DISCUSSION QUESTIONS

1. Why is the attitude of the Christian toward death one of mixed feelings? How is this reflected in the average funeral service of a Christian?

2. What do we know happens to the Christian immediately after death? The non-Christian?

3. God's Word leaves many of our questions about death unanswered. What are some of your unanswered questions about the nature of death? If God does not answer them in Scripture, how do you handle them?

54

The Resurrection

INTRODUCTION

For the Christian, the soul lives on in heaven after death until it is reunited with the body at the second coming of Christ. In this lesson, Dr. Sproul teaches the future hope of the resurrection of the body for the Christian and the nature of our glorified resurrected bodies.

MESSAGE OVERVIEW

I. What is the meaning of the word *resurrection*?
   a. The Greek word simply means "to rise again." But the word takes on deeper theological significance in the way the New Testament uses it.
   b. "We believe in the resurrection of the body," the phrase from the Apostles' Creed, does not refer to the raising of Christ but ourselves. In our case, we are confessing that our bodies, while undergoing the corruption of the grave, nevertheless will be raised and glorified in the Last Day.

II. What is the biblical teaching concerning this resurrection?
   a. In Romans 8:11, Paul says that since Christ has been raised from the dead, we will be changed. Is that change simply spiritual, or is this referring to our final resurrection? He goes on to make reference to the raising of Jesus' mortal body, and then compares that raising to ours. This is not a reference only to the spirit—it is a reference to the body, as well.
   b. The New Testament does not view the Resurrection as an isolated event. Jesus' raising is the first of many.
   c. Was Jesus the first to be resurrected? Yes, because all others who were raised from the dead eventually died. Jesus rose to never perish, and this points to the change that takes place at resurrection.

d. There are many similarities between the resurrection of Jesus and the raisings of others in the Bible—but the main difference is that Jesus' body underwent radical changes to become a glorified body.

III. The main doctrinal passage in the Bible concerning the Resurrection is 1 Corinthians 15.

a. Following Zeno, Paul uses the *reductio ad absurdum* argument against those who oppose the doctrine of the Resurrection.
b. Paul shows that you cannot have the Christian faith without the doctrine of the Resurrection. Some theologians claim that you can have Christianity without a supernatural emphasis, such as the Resurrection. Bultmann gives an excellent explanation of the doctrine as taught by Paul, but denies its truth.
c. The apostle Paul does not base his case simply on the problems that come from not having a Resurrection. This method of argument is common today, but it proves nothing. Paul goes on to appeal to eyewitnesses, including his own account of seeing Jesus on the road to Damascus.
d. In 1 Corinthians 15:35, the question is asked, "What will our bodies in heaven look like?" Paul says he does not know. But he makes an analogy to nature (following Plato) to argue that what we will look like will resemble our former bodies in the way a tree resembles the seed from which it grew. There will be some continuity, but there will be significant discontinuity.
e. Will our bodies look like Jesus' in the Upper Room? Was His the prototype, or did it have further glorification to attain when He ascended? We do not know.
f. We will be immortal in heaven. But will we be inherently immortal? No. We will remain sustained by God. God guarantees our immortality, not our own strength.
g. The highest form of life is not what we see now. The apex of human life is still in the future.
h. We will be like Jesus, receiving the same glorious resurrection as He received.

STUDY QUESTIONS

1. What does *resurrection* mean?
   a. To rise again
   b. To conquer death
   c. To not die
   d. To continue living

2. Christ's bodily resurrection from the dead was an isolated event.
   a. True
   b. False

3. If Christ raised people from the dead, how can we say Christ was the first person to experience resurrection?
   a. Because those people never actually died
   b. Because Christ didn't have to die again
   c. Because Christ didn't raise anyone from the dead
   d. Because Christ didn't actually die

4. What type of body did Christ have after His resurrection?
   a. He had a recognizable body.
   b. He had the same body.
   c. He had a glorified body.
   d. He did not have a body.

5. The Christian faith is nonexistent apart from ______.
   a. Faith
   b. Works
   c. Purification
   d. Christ's resurrection

6. After death, what will our heavenly bodies still be?
   a. Sinful
   b. Mortal
   c. Human
   d. Recognizable

DISCUSSION QUESTIONS

1. Summarize Paul's argument for the resurrection of the body.

2. What is the relationship between Jesus's resurrection and ours?

55

The Kingdom of God

INTRODUCTION

The coming of Christ was the inauguration of the kingdom of God, which will be fully manifest at the end of time. In this lesson, Dr. Sproul explains the nature of God's kingdom and the fundamental task of the church in relation to it.

MESSAGE OVERVIEW

I. Introduction
   a. "Until kingdom come" is a casual expression about something that has permanence.
   b. The Lord's Prayer explains what this phrase means. The kingdom has come and His will is being done, even now in heaven. But in this world, this is not true in the same way.
   c. God's kingdom is universal and eternal. But the voluntary submission of creatures to God is in process. This is clear since Old Testament times.
   d. The kingdom of heaven is not different from the kingdom of God. Matthew was writing to Jews and he did not want to offend them by using the name of God. So he circumlocuted God's name, using the term "heaven" to represent God's name.
   e. The kingdom of God is not totally in the future. The biblical evidence is overwhelming about this.
   f. In the New Testament, the kingdom of God is said to be at hand. Jesus illustrates this through His "party" attitude. The King is in your midst, so rejoice!

II. How do we make visible the invisible kingdom?
   a. First, by being Christ's witnesses here.
   b. Second, by living out His Lordship over us now.
   c. Third, by looking to the future consummation of the kingdom.

III. The progressive character of the kingdom is illustrated in the parables.
   a. "The kingdom of God is like a mustard seed."
   b. "The kingdom of God is like bread growing."
   c. "Seek first the kingdom of God, and His righteousness."
   d. Just because the kingdom is invisible does not mean it is unreal.

STUDY QUESTIONS

1. Where did the expression "till kingdom come" originate?
   a. From the Lord's Prayer
   b. During times of war
   c. In reference to a building
   d. From a popular hymn

2. What is the unifying theme of the Bible?
   a. The coming of the Messiah
   b. The kingdom of God
   c. The victory of Christ
   d. The promise of the covenant

3. The kingdom of God is something that is completely in the future.
   a. True
   b. False

4. Why did John the Baptist's disciples fast while Jesus' disciples did not?
   a. They were more spiritual.
   b. They were more holy.
   c. They were more faithful.
   d. They were waiting for Jesus.

5. What is the fundamental task of the church?
   a. To restore cultural dominion
   b. To gain political power
   c. To bear witness to the kingdom of God
   d. To drive out God's enemies

6. By what means did Jesus teach the progressive nature of the kingdom of God?
   a. Through psalms
   b. Through prayer
   c. Through miracles
   d. Through parables

DISCUSSION QUESTIONS

1. In what sense is the kingdom of God present? In what sense is the kingdom of God future?

2. Is the kingdom of heaven different from the kingdom of God?

3. In what ways do we make the invisible kingdom visible?

4. What are some of the biblical passages that illustrate the progressive character of the kingdom of God?

56

The Millennium

INTRODUCTION

The millennium is the thousand-year reign of Jesus Christ, a period which has been interpreted with much variation. In this lesson, Dr. Sproul discusses the various views regarding the order and nature of the millennial reign of Christ.

MESSAGE OVERVIEW

I. The idea of the Millennium is very controversial. Dr. Sproul has changed his position repeatedly and is not dogmatic at almost any point.
   a. Why? It is because of the nature and genre of the literature in which our facts about the Millennium are found. See Revelation 20 for details on the one thousand-year binding of Satan.
   b. The two basic issues concern its nature and it chronology.
   c. Millennial views are described via prefixes, such as premillenial or postmillenial.

II. How do we read prophetic or apocalyptic literature?
   a. To interpret it literally means that we interpret it as it was intended, not that we interpret it the way we read epistles. Figurative sections of Scripture should be read like poetry; that is "literally" the correct way to interpret them.
   b. Consistency is very difficult for those who espouse a "literal at all cost" way of reading Scripture.

III. The various millennial views are quite distinct.
   a. Premillennialism sees the many events of the last days occurring prior to the one thousand-year reign of Christ and the corresponding binding of Satan.
      i. Historic premillennialism
      ii. Dispensational premillennialism

b. Amillennialism does not see a literal one thousand-year period in Revelation 20.
c. Postmillennialism sees Christ returning after the events of the last days, and coming to a victorious church rather than a decadent one, countering dispensational premillennialism.

IV. Preterism
a. Full preterism teaches that all predicted events in the New Testament occurred prior to A.D. 100.
b. Partial preterism teaches that many of the prophecies have come true, and that the first 20 chapters of Revelation have been accomplished.

STUDY QUESTIONS

1. What is the most highly debated topic of eschatology?
   a. Theonomy
   b. The millennium
   c. Dispensationalism
   d. The binding of Satan

2. What do the prefixes of millennial positions differentiate?
   a. The nature of the millennium
   b. The timing of the millennium
   c. The events of the millennium
   d. The signs of the millennium

3. What does literalism in interpretation mean?
   a. To apply a literal interpretation to figurative imagery
   b. To interpret Scripture according to its genre
   c. To ignore spiritual analogy
   d. To interpret future prophecies literally

4. What problem does a reader face when interpreting Revelation?
   a. Its genre
   b. Its chronology
   c. Its reliability
   d. Its brutality

5. Which millennial position is also a complete system of doctrine?
   a. Historic premillennialism
   b. Dispensationalism
   c. Amillennialism
   d. Postmillennialism

6. What does dispensationalism teach that is different from the other millennial positions?
   a. Christ will come back after the millennium concludes.
   b. There should be a literal interpretation of future prophecies.
   c. God has two separate plans of redemption.
   d. There will be no literal millennium.

DISCUSSION QUESTIONS

1. What is the definition of premillennialism? Amillennialism? Postmillennialism?

2. What is the predominant eschatology in evangelicalism today?

3. What is the difference between partial preterism and full preterism?

4. What event do preterists believe Matthew 24 and much of Revelation predicted?

57

The Return of Christ

INTRODUCTION

The return of Jesus has often been a source of controversy. Many have tried to determine when Christ will return even though Christ Himself revealed that no one knows the day or the hour of His return. In this lesson, Dr. Sproul mentions three aspects of the second coming of Christ that we can know.

MESSAGE OVERVIEW

I. Karl Barth observed in 1949 that Christians should be reading the Bible in one hand and the newspaper in the other. This comment was sparked by the rise of the modern state of Israel.

II. Jesus predicted that Jerusalem would be occupied until the "times of the Gentiles" were fulfilled.
   a. In Romans 11, Paul uses this phrase as he discusses the question, "What about Israel?"
   b. The events in this century have made some say that we are in the final days. The expectations of the return of Jesus are at a fever pitch.
   c. This is something for us to place our hope in, but the questions of how and when Jesus will return is an ongoing debate.

III. The Ascension teaches us much about the return of Christ (Acts 1).
   a. "Men of Galilee, why do you stand staring up into heaven?"
   b. The return of Christ will be personal, visible, and glorious.

IV. The crisis of the parousia is caused by the apparent delay in Jesus' predicted return.
   a. According to nineteenth century critics, Jesus was disappointed that God did not vindicate His efforts.

b. "My God, My God, why hast Thou forsaken Me?"
c. Others, such as C.H. Dodd, have said that all the prophecies of the New Testament were fulfilled in the first century.
d. "This generation will not pass away until all these things are fulfilled."
e. It seems as if Jesus was correct that the temple would fall and that Jerusalem would not perish. But did Jesus return 40 years after His prediction?
f. Evangelicals have responded to this by saying that the word *generation* does not refer to a time frame but to a type of people. "This kind of people will be around when I return," is a possible meaning, but unlikely.
g. Other evangelicals have said that "all these things" refers only to the first two events.
h. Full preterism teaches that Jesus' return occurred in A.D. 70. The Jewish age ended and the age of the Gentiles began. Many hold to a secret Rapture and a hidden resurrection that happened in A.D. 70.
i. The return of Christ in A.D. 70 was but a typological fulfillment, though. It was a foretaste of His great future coming, just as many prophesied events are fulfilled typologically soon after the prediction, only to be fulfilled truly at a later date.

STUDY QUESTIONS

1. What is "the blessed hope of the people of God"?
   a. The return of Christ
   b. No more suffering
   c. Seeing loved ones again
   d. The resurrection of the body

2. Christ's return will be personal, visible, and in glory.
   a. True
   b. False

3. What does realized eschatology teach?
   a. Christ's future predictions are unreliable.
   b. Future prophecies were fulfilled in the first century.
   c. Christ's return took place in the first century.
   d. Jesus expected an earthly kingdom and died in disillusionment.

4. When was the temple and Jerusalem destroyed?
   a. AD 70
   b. AD 50
   c. AD 40
   d. AD 30

5. According to the lecture, how Jesus use the word *generation*?
   a. In reference to all of Israel
   b. In reference to the first generation of Christians
   c. In reference to a single human generation
   d. In reference to the lifetime of the twelve disciples

6. Which theory teaches Christ returned in AD 70?
   a. Realized eschatology
   b. Full preterism
   c. Hyper-Calvinism
   d. Typological fulfillment

DISCUSSION QUESTIONS

1. What do we learn about the return of Christ from the record of the ascension of Christ in Acts 1?

2. What is the crisis of the parousia?

3. What are some of the explanations of Jesus' phrase "this generation" in Matthew 24:34?

4. What is the relationship between the judgment coming of Christ in A.D. 70 and His coming in glory at the end of the age?

58

The Final Judgment

INTRODUCTION

When we stop to think about all that we have said and done in our lives and how God will judge us, it is sobering to say the least. How should we, as Christians, view the final judgment? In this lesson, Dr. Sproul builds on our understanding of the final judgment and explains why those who are in Christ do not need to fear judgment.

MESSAGE OVERVIEW

I. Nietzsche announced in the nineteenth century that God had died. Humanism prepared the world to believe that we do not need God.
   a. Civilization is divided into three phases, according to Compte—infancy, adolescence, and adulthood.
   b. World War I was supposed to be the "War to end all wars."
   c. In all this was the "good" news that since God does not exist, we do not have to worry about facing divine judgment.
   d. Life and death were both meaningless. Optimism was turned to gloom.

II. The New Testament teaches that life and death are real and meaningful. But that means that accountability is a reality.
   a. In Acts 17, Paul declares to the Gentiles a God who, in former times of ignorance, was more tolerant. But a critical change has occurred and all men everywhere will be judged in light of the coming of Christ. Since this watershed event has occurred, God will judge unrepentance much more harshly.
   b. The Old Testament warned of the Day of the Lord, a day of great judgment.
   c. Kant said that every human being has a sense of "oughtness" built into his or her mind. This sense is the foundation of his argument for the existence of God. His argument demands divine judgment.
   d. Our own minds record our sin. But all our deeds also are located in the mind of God.

III. In Matthew's gospel, Jesus ends His sermon on the Mount in a dramatic fashion.
   a. "Every tree that does not bear good fruit is cut down and thrown into the fire."
   b. We will be judged and rewarded or punished according to our works.
   c. In Matthew 25, Jesus teaches that He will judge men who pretend to love and serve Him. The parable of the ten virgins is used to illustrate this truth.
   d. These warnings concerning final judgment must be heeded. They are among Jesus' most fearful teachings.

STUDY QUESTIONS

1. Who announced the supposed death of God in the nineteenth century?
   a. Søren Kierkegaard
   b. Friedrich Nietzsche
   c. Ludwig Wittgenstein
   d. Immanuel Kant

2. According to the positivist movement, what is the stage of adulthood in Western civilization?
   a. History
   b. Religion
   c. Philosophy
   d. Science

3. Deep down, what does every human know?
   a. Nothing matters.
   b. Everyone will be held accountable by God.
   c. Good people go to heaven based on their actions.
   d. Morality is a product of evolutionary development.

4. Which philosopher taught that people have a sense of "oughtness"?
   a. Immanuel Kant
   b. René Descartes
   c. Søren Kierkegaard
   d. Friedrich Nietzsche

5. Where do we first get the idea of the day of judgment?
   a. From Paul
   b. From Jesus
   c. From the Apostles
   d. From the Old Testament

6. When Jesus spoke of the final judgment, according to what did He say every person will be judged?
   a. According to their works
   b. According to their faith
   c. According to their church attendance
   d. According to their care of the poor

DISCUSSION QUESTIONS

1. What does Acts 17 teach about the judgment of God?

2. What do we learn about God's judgment in the Sermon on the Mount?

3. What does Matthew 25 teach about the final judgment?

59

Eternal Punishment

INTRODUCTION

The doctrine of hell is an unpopular teaching today, but that doesn't change the fact that it is still a biblical teaching. We serve a holy God, and His just demands will not allow sin to go unpunished. In this lesson, Dr. Sproul defends the doctrine of hell as a just penalty for sin, a penalty that we all deserve apart from Christ.

MESSAGE OVERVIEW

I. Jesus affirms the reality of a future judgment. But what happens after judgment? There is a verdict and—for the unredeemed—a penalty.
   a. God is the perfect judge. He will judge us on the basis of works—either ours or Christ's.
   b. No person has been or ever will be judged unjustly by God.
   c. "If the Lord should mark iniquity, who would stand?"
   d. No person ever can say he had no idea about God and His basic requirements. Romans 1 teaches that men suppress the clear knowledge of God and His higher attributes.
   e. People will not be judged for rejecting Jesus if people have not actually rejected Him. But they will be judged for rejecting the Father, whom they do know.

II. Our destiny is unalterable after judgment.
   - It is appointed for man once to die, and then judgment. There is no purgatory.

III. The doctrine of hell is one of great difficulty.
   a. How can we be eternally happy in heaven knowing that our mother or wife is in hell?
   b. Our basic affections are rooted in this world. In heaven, we will be sanctified enough to love the vindication of the righteousness of God.

c. Even in our most righteous moments, we are much closer to Hitler than Jesus.
d. Hell is so bad that we would not believe in it for a moment except that Jesus taught so clearly about it.

IV. Revelation 20 gives us an image of hell that, while poetic, has a frightening clarity.
a. Is hell literally a lake of fire? Probably not. But do not be relieved.
b. The lake of fire imagery is just the worst thing that Jesus could use to describe it. The people in hell may be praying that they could have the pleasure of resting in a lake of fire. The reality must be worse than the symbol.

V. What is the nature of hell?
a. It is not separation from God's presence but separation from the graces of God.
b. There are degrees of punishment in hell. God is a perfect judge.
c. It is not a place of annihilation. This ancient heresy has seen a revival in our time, but Scripture remains clear—conscious, eternal punishment is reserved for those who die in unbelief.

VI. Objection: How could God punish a finite person with infinite punishment? Because this finite person has committed the ultimate offense against God.

STUDY QUESTIONS

1. Since not everyone has heard about Christ, there are innocent people who do not deserve punishment.
   a. True
   b. False

2. How will the person who never hears the gospel be judged?
   a. According to the gospel itself
   b. According to special revelation
   c. According to his good works alone
   d. According to the light that he has received

3. Who taught on the subject of hell the most in Scripture?
   a. Jesus
   b. Paul
   c. Peter
   d. John the Baptist

4. What is the most common scriptural description of hell?
   a. As a den of lions
   b. As a lake of fire
   c. As a bottomless pit
   d. As a pit of snakes

5. What are we ultimately saved from?
   a. Hell
   b. Our sin
   c. Ourselves
   d. God's wrath

6. Which doctrine makes hell obsolete?
   a. Conscious eternal torment
   b. Annihilationism
   c. Soul sleep
   d. Purgatory

DISCUSSION QUESTIONS

1. Is mankind judged on the basis of works? Explain.

2. Will those who never have heard of Jesus be judged for rejecting Jesus?

3. How can we be joyful in heaven knowing that loved ones are in hell?

4. Is hell a literal lake of fire?

5. What biblical evidence do we have that implies that there are degrees of punishment in hell?

6. What is the doctrine of annihilationism?

60

The Believer's Final Rest

INTRODUCTION

There are many things about heaven that have not been revealed to us. Yet, we know that in heaven Christians will experience a rest that none of us have experienced in this life. In this lesson, Dr. Sproul describes what to expect when we reach the final destination of the Christian life.

MESSAGE OVERVIEW

I. What happens at the end of the Christian life?
   a. Each Sunday, we experience the Sabbath rest, which foreshadows the coming eternal rest.
   b. Modernists deny the reality of heaven, asking on what basis we have any confidence as to the nature of the next life.
   c. When Lazarus died, Jesus took the opportunity to teach by saying to Martha, "I am the resurrection and the life. He who believes in Me, though he may die, he shall live" (John 11:25).

II. In John 14, Jesus teaches that we are not to worry about our future in heaven or the exact nature of the afterlife.
   a. At the Last Supper, in the Upper Room, Jesus makes a point to address the fears of His disciples.
   b. "If it were not so, I would have told you" (John 14:2).
   c. Jesus has prepared a place for His people. We have every reason to be confident of its reality.
   d. In 1 John 3:1–2, a key eschatological passage in the New Testament, we discover that whatever our exact nature in heaven, we will be, in important respects, like Christ in His glorified state.

III. The beatific vision of God (*visio Dei*) is one of the great promises He makes to His people.
   a. "Beatific" is not an ordinary word to us, but words like *Beatitudes* are. The message of Christ in Matthew 5 gave the hearers great blessings and promises, a degree of pleasure that transcends any happiness we could experience on earth.
   b. The vision itself carries with it a great blessing. As John says, we don't know what we will be like, but by seeing God, we will be blessed to such a degree that we will be like Him.
   c. The Old Testament says that there is a limit: No man can see God. Even Moses, who begged to see Him, was not allowed to see God. The intimate vision of God was forbidden.
   d. One of the hardest things about the Christian life is that we serve an invisible God.
   e. If God is invisible, how can we see Him in the first place? Notice the Beatitude that says, "Blessed are the pure in heart, for they shall see God." When we receive the fullness of our sanctification, the barrier of sin will be removed.
   f. But how can we see a spirit? Great thinkers have struggled with how the Christian will see God. The illustration of the difference between watching televised events and real events helps us understand this.
   g. What we will have in heaven is spirit-to-spirit communication. We don't know how that will work, but it helps us understand how we can "see" an invisible, spiritual God.

IV. In Revelation 21, we get another vision of the nature of the afterlife.
   a. When the Bible talks about heaven, it focuses on some odd things, things that will be there and things that will not be there. We assume these are symbolic representations, given the nature of this kind of literature, but it should not surprise us if God does have a lavish place prepared for us.
   b. Why no sea? The sea represented violence and catastrophe.
   c. There will be no tears. In this case, this means there will be no sadness.
   d. In verse 22 and following, we learn that there will be no sun or temple or moon. Is this a dark place? Or a place without a church?
   e. God's heaven will be full of Him. He will fulfill everything that was just a shadow of Himself.

STUDY QUESTIONS

1. How do we experience a taste of heaven on earth?
   a. Through doing good deeds
   b. Through Sabbath rest
   c. Through fellowship
   d. Through prayer

2. Which of the following reasons for which Jesus ascended to heaven is a great comfort for believers who are about to enter their final rest?
   a. Jesus promised that He has prepared a place for us.
   b. Jesus has taken His seat at the right hand of the Father.
   c. Jesus sends the Holy Spirit as a Comforter for His people.
   d. Jesus enjoys His preincarnate glory with the Father.

3. What did Dr. Sproul say is possibly the most important eschatological text in the New Testament?
   a. The millennial reign of Christ in Revelation 20
   b. The Sermon on the Mount in Matthew 5
   c. The Olivet Discourse in Matthew 24
   d. The beatific vision in 1 John 3

4. What did Jonathan Edwards believe about our vision of God in heaven?
   a. Our hearts will perceive God fully.
   b. Our eyes will be blinded by the light of God.
   c. Our souls will have a direct vision of God.
   d. Our vision of God will be mediated through our eyes.

5. What concept is directly tied with the beatific vision?
   a. Intimacy
   b. Luminescence
   c. Blessedness
   d. Beauty

6. What does the sea represent in Hebrew poetry?
   a. Sorrow
   b. Satan
   c. Violence
   d. Peace

DISCUSSION QUESTIONS

1. How does the Sabbath act as a foretaste of heaven? How does that give us direction on how to "keep the Sabbath"?

2. What is the beatific vision? How is it a blessing?

3. How can we "see" an invisible God?

4. According to Revelation 21, heaven is filled with things we would not expect, but absent of things very common to us today. What is the final image we get of heaven from Scripture? What about it surprises you?

ANSWER KEY FOR STUDY QUESTIONS

Lesson 1
1. B
2. A
3. B
4. B
5. D
6. A

Lesson 2
1. A
2. B
3. B
4. D
5. A
6. D

Lesson 3
1. A
2. B
3. B
4. B
5. A
6. B

Lesson 4
1. A.
2. B
3. A
4. D
5. D
6. B

Lesson 5
1. B
2. A
3. B
4. D
5. A
6. A

Lesson 6
1. D
2. B
3. D
4. B
5. C
6. B

Lesson 7
1. A
2. B
3. C
4. B
5. B
6. A

Lesson 8
1. C
2. B
3. A
4. A
5. B
6. B

Lesson 9
1. D
2. B
3. B
4. C
5. D
6. A

Lesson 10
1. B
2. B
3. D
4. C
5. D
6. D

Lesson 11
1. B
2. A
3. D
4. B
5. A
6. D

Lesson 12
1. C
2. B
3. A
4. D
5. D
6. D

Lesson 13
1. B
2. D
3. D
4. C
5. B
6. A

Lesson 14
1. B
2. B
3. D
4. A
5. D
6. B

Lesson 15
1. B
2. B
3. C
4. D
5. B
6. C

Lesson 16
1. D
2. B
3. D
4. C
5. A
6. C

Lesson 17
1. D
2. C
3. B
4. A
5. C
6. B

Lesson 18
1. B
2. A
3. C
4. B
5. A
6. D

Lesson 19
1. B
2. D
3. A
4. B
5. A
6. D

Lesson 20
1. B
2. B
3. D
4. A
5. C
6. A

Lesson 21
1. B
2. C
3. A
4. C
5. A
6. A

Lesson 22
1. A
2. C
3. A
4. B
5. C
6. D

Lesson 23
1. B
2. D
3. B
4. B
5. A
6. A

Lesson 24
1. A
2. A
3. D
4. B
5. C
6. D

Lesson 25
1. B
2. C
3. C
4. B
5. C
6. A

Lesson 26
1. A
2. B
3. D
4. D
5. C
6. B

Lesson 27
1. B
2. A
3. C
4. B
5. B
6. B

Lesson 28
1. D
2. B
3. B
4. A
5. A
6. A

Lesson 29
1. C
2. B
3. A
4. A
5. C
6. C

Lesson 30
1. B
2. C
3. B
4. B
5. D
6. B

Lesson 31
1. A
2. A
3. D
4. B
5. D
6. A

Lesson 32
1. A
2. C
3. A
4. A
5. D
6. D

Lesson 33
1. B
2. D
3. A
4. A
5. B
6. D

Lesson 34
1. A
2. B
3. D
4. C
5. A
6. B

Lesson 35
1. D
2. B
3. A
4. D
5. D
6. B

Lesson 36
1. B
2. A
3. C
4. D
5. A
6. D

Lesson 37
1. D
2. C
3. A
4. B
5. B
6. B

Lesson 38
1. D
2. B
3. B
4. C
5. D
6. B

Lesson 39
1. B
2. A
3. D
4. B
5. A
6. A

Lesson 40
1. A
2. B
3. C
4. D
5. A
6. A

Lesson 41
1. A
2. B
3. D
4. B
5. B
6. A

Lesson 42
1. C
2. A
3. B
4. A
5. A
6. D

Lesson 43
1. D
2. A
3. B
4. B
5. A
6. D

Lesson 44
1. C
2. B
3. A
4. B
5. A
6. C

Lesson 45
1. B
2. D
3. C
4. A
5. B
6. D

Lesson 46
1. B
2. D
3. A
4. C
5. D
6. A

Lesson 47
1. C
2. B
3. B
4. C
5. A
6. A

Lesson 48
1. B
2. D
3. B
4. A
5. B
6. D

Lesson 49
1. B
2. A
3. C
4. C
5. B
6. C

Lesson 50
1. B
2. A
3. B
4. B
5. C
6. D

Lesson 51
1. B
2. C
3. B
4. C
5. B
6. A

Lesson 52

1. C
2. A
3. A
4. C
5. B
6. C

Lesson 53

1. A
2. C
3. B
4. A
5. B
6. C

Lesson 54

1. A
2. B
3. B
4. C
5. D
6. C

Lesson 55

1. A
2. B
3. B
4. D
5. C
6. D

Lesson 56

1. B
2. B
3. B
4. A
5. B
6. C

Lesson 57

1. A
2. A
3. B
4. A
5. C
6. B

Lesson 58

1. B
2. D
3. B
4. A
5. D
6. A

Lesson 59

1. B
2. D
3. A
4. B
5. D
6. B

Lesson 60

1. B
2. A
3. D
4. C
5. C
6. C

ANSWER EXPLANATIONS

LESSON 1

1. The combination of the Greek words *theos* (God) and *logos* (word) produce the word we know as *theology*. While theology proper narrowly refers to the study of God Himself, the study of theology looks at all of those things that God has revealed to us in sacred Scripture.

2. All disciplines of study are to be understood in light of the overarching reality of the character of God. Because God is the source of all truth, and He has revealed Himself to us, it would be foolishness not to study what He has said.

3. The goal of theology is not to squeeze the Bible into our predetermined frameworks, but to organize and systematize its teachings in a way that is faithful to the character and Word of God.

4. Explanation: While it is true that God's Word is living and active (Heb. 4:12), Dr. Sproul mentioned these four assumptions: (1) God has revealed Himself to His creation, (2) God's Word is rationally consistent, (3) God is not the author of chaos, and (4) God's Word is unified. Without all four, the attempt to systematize the teaching of Scripture becomes a fool's errand.

5. One of the most influential philosophies to emerge in Western history has been the philosophy known as existentialism, which presupposes that there is no such thing as essential truth. The existentialist believes that we are cast into a world that is ultimately chaotic and is without meaning and purpose, in opposition to systematic theology which seeks to find order and purpose in God's revelation.

6. One point in theology addresses every other point in theology. The task of the systematic theologian is to see how all of the pieces of divine revelation fit together into an organic, meaningful, consistent, and coherent whole.

LESSON 2

1. While theologians have been dealing with the same text for the past 2,000 years, modern scholarship may yield nuances to certain Greek and Hebrew words that

were not available to past theologians. These nuances will give better insight into the text, while not changing the organic system of the Bible.

2. Theology was formerly known as the "queen of the sciences," since science is the ultimate quest for *knowledge*. Though working on different levels, the biologist seeks knowledge about living organisms, and the theologian seeks knowledge about God Himself.

3. While theology certainly deals with the practical, the three spheres which Dr. Sproul mentions are biblical theology, historical theology, and systematic theology. The systematician relies on the insights of biblical theology, as well as the doctrinal development of historical theology, in order to present a complete picture of Scripture's teachings.

4. Every time a Christian speaks about the Lord Jesus, they are doing theology whether they realize it or not. The Christian should desire to be accurate in their knowledge of Christ and to study Scripture in order to grow in obedience and maturity (2 Tim. 3:16).

5. The Bible is the chief and principal source for the study of systematic theology. While other theological disciplines may interact and influence the systematician, systematic theology is primarily rooted in God's Word.

6. Atomism seeks to study only parts of Scripture in exclusion from the rest of the Bible. This discipline does not consider the biblical writers to be inspired and puts the authors against each other, saying that each Apostle had a different theology.

LESSON 3

1. General revelation is given to all humans at all times. God's general revelation is made to humans in the created world and in the conscience of the human heart. God has put enough revelation of Himself in nature and in the conscience so as to leave man without excuse (Rom. 1:20).

2. Augustine uses the analogy of eyesight to explain truth. Though we may have perfect eyesight, we cannot see unless there is light. Similarly, we cannot come to a knowledge of the truth apart from it being revealed to us by God.

3. General revelation can also be called natural revelation. Though they overlap, general revelation is properly God's (objective) revelation of Himself universally in nature, while natural theology is that which is actually revealed (subjectively) to the natural man, what God allows to enter our minds.

4. Because of the effects of the fall, our hearts and minds are sinful. As natural men, any understanding we have of God (natural theology) is therefore distorted.

However, this fact does not mean that God's revelation in nature (general revelation) is flawed—on the contrary, it is perfect.

5. Christianity is not based upon someone's speculative philosophy, but stands or falls as a revealed faith. The fundamental assertion of the Christian faith is that the truth that we embrace as Christians is truth that has come to us from God Himself.

6. Paul says, "what may be known of God is manifest in them; for God has shown it to them." He uses the word that, in Latin, is *manifestum*; in the Greek, it's *phaneros*, and the idea is that God has not planted these esoteric clues under rocks and in caves, but that the revelation that He gives of Himself is *manifestum*—it's clear.

LESSON 4

1. A medium is a means or intermediary through which something is communicated. When we talk about mediate general revelation, we talk about that revelation that God gives of Himself through a medium other than Himself. Scripture is an example of mediate revelation, whereas His immediate revelation is the inward work of the Holy Spirit bearing witness to us about its truth and authority.

2. Theophany—an outward manifestation of God—is an example of extra-Scriptural special revelation. While there are numerous accounts of God revealing Himself to His people, the most famous is His appearing to Moses in the burning bush.

3. The biggest problem that Israel struggled with in her history was with the false prophets who were known for teaching things the people wanted to hear rather than the true revelation that came from God. God gave the people tests to determine whether a prophet was truly from Him, including call, miracles, and fulfillment of prophecy.

4. We have the Bible, which gives us God's special revelation, but we also have the Word of God incarnate, whom we learn about through the written Word. The one who embodies the very Word of God is Jesus Himself, as Jesus told His disciples, "Whoever has seen me has seen the Father" (John 14:9). Jesus Christ is the supreme revelation of God to us.

5. In the New Testament, the counterpart to the prophet is the Apostle. The chief criterion of an Apostle in the New Testament was that an Apostle was called directly and immediately by Christ, because to be an Apostle means to be one who is sent or commissioned with the authority of the one who is sending them.

6. One of the controversies in the New Testament is that Paul was not one of the original disciples, did not know Jesus during Jesus' earthly ministry, was not an eyewitness of the resurrection like the rest of them were, and so seems to lack the credentials necessary to be an Apostle. That is why Paul often records the circumstances of his call on the road to Damascus and is confirmed by the other Apostles.

LESSON 5

1. A primary issue in conflict during the Reformation was authority. The Roman Catholic Church placed councils, creeds, and Scripture on the same level of authority, but the Reformers argued that councils, creeds, and confessions are subservient to the supreme authority of Scripture.

2. All Scripture is breathed out by God through divine inspiration. God superintends the writing of sacred Scripture through the Holy Spirit. God does not just act and let people respond with their own insight and their own imagination to set forth their view of what God has done. Rather, the Holy Spirit superintends the record to make sure that what is written is His Word.

3. Some people have charged orthodox Christianity with teaching mechanical inspiration, or the dictation theory of inspiration. Mechanical inspiration is the view that when God inspired Scripture, He used the human authors like a pen in His hand, overriding their humanity.

4. The Bible does not explain to us the precise manner in which God inspired His Word to be written, but it does tell us that men spoke from God as they were carried along by the Holy Spirit (2 Peter 1:21). God superintended the writing of sacred Scripture, using the personalities, vocabularies, and concerns of the human writers to write His Word without error.

5. Throughout history, the church has been zealous to reconstruct as carefully as possible the original manuscripts of the Bible, giving much care to studying the word meanings of ancient Hebrew and Greek terms. Inspiration does not simply apply to the broad outline of the information communicated by the earthly authors, but rather to the very words of Scripture themselves.

6. Jesus' view of inspiration was more detailed and specific than being verbal; it was jot-and-tittle inspiration of our Lord, saying that there is not a word in the law of God that is superfluous or that is open to negotiation. All of Scripture carries with it the weight of the binding authority of its ultimate Author.

LESSON 6

1. Conservative Christians refer to the Bile as the "only infallible rule for faith and practice" but liberal Christians refer to it as "infallible" *only* when speaking about faith and practice. Using the word *only* this way is called limited inerrancy, which has become very popular in our day.

2. *Infallible* means unable to err or make mistakes, and to be inerrant is to actually be without error. Therefore, if something is infallible, it must also be inerrant.

3. To be wrong about something, even if it is unintentional, is to bear false witness, which is a violation of the ninth commandment. If Jesus is wrong, then He is not sinless and is disqualified from being our Savior.

4. If the Bible gives inaccurate or false information about miracles, morality, science, or history, then we have lost our basis for believing anything that it says, even about Christ Himself.

5. The Bible is the only infallible rule of faith and practice because it has been delegated by the only Lord of the church. This is the view of Scripture taught by Jesus Himself. It is infallible and authoritative for all of life because it is God's Word. It is infallible because it, like God, cannot err and inerrant because it is without error.

6. One of the complaints to the doctrine of inerrancy is that it was the creation of 17th century protestant scholasticism, and that the idea of inerrancy was a rational construct that was foreign to the biblical writers themselves and to the Magisterial Reformers of the 16th century. However, Martin Luther stated that the Scriptures do not err, and the early church fathers possessed the same sympathies.

LESSON 7

1. The question of canon has to do with which books are Scripture and, thus, should be included in the Bible. The early church had to wrestle with the question of which writings constitute the New Testament Scriptures.

2. The Roman Catholic Church considers the books of the Apocrypha to be Scripture, but the Protestants examined the issue of canonicity and determined that the Apocrypha did not have the marks of Apostolic authority, and other marks of canonicity.

3. Though critics point out that the canon of Scripture was not complete for hundreds of years, there was already a functional canon operating before it was formally codified by the church. The basic books of the New Testament that we read and observe today were in use in the life of the church, and they functioned as canon because of their Apostolic authority from the very beginning.

4. The Protestant view recognizes that the church makes mistakes in history (i.e., the Apocrypha) and therefore believes that we have a fallible collection of infallible books. However, this fact should not discourage us, for God providentially cares for His church and is guarding His Word for us today.

5. The heretic Marcion believed that the God of the Old Testament was a lesser deity who was fierce and angry, and what Christ came to do in the New Testament was to reveal the true God. Marcion created his own canon where he abandoned the Old

Testament and cut up most of the New Testament. The church's response to this heresy was to give an authoritative formal list of actual biblical books.

6. The threefold test that was used in order to determine canonical authenticity included Apostolic origin, church reception, and doctrinal continuity. Even though there was historical search and investigation, we can be fully assured that God made sure that the right books were included in the canon of sacred Scripture.

LESSON 8

1. Because the Roman Catholic Church invests the same level of authority in Scripture and church tradition, they refer to them as the dual source of revelation from God.

2. Though the wording that explicitly put Scripture and the church on the same level of authority was made more ambiguous, we know from later Roman Catholic decrees and writings that Trent was not a repudiation of the "dual-source" doctrine.

3. The early church didn't believe that they created the biblical canon. They used the phrase "we receive" acknowledging that they were not the source of God's revelation, but rather the recipients of it. The church was not so arrogant as to claim that they were creating the canon or that the canon derived its authority from the authority of the church.

4. When we come to the Bible we are receiving the gracious revelation of God to man. It is thus the authority to be submitted to, not something which we can stand in judgment over. This is humbling to sinful human pride.

5. The church is always subordinate to the authority of the Bible, but this does not mean that the church has no authority. State governments and parents have authority, but they are authorities that are delegated by God. Even though we need to respect and obey it, church authority is subordinate to the authority of Scripture itself.

6. Prolegomena deals with the first things or principles before the study of theology can commence such as dating, culture, and language. A problem with too much background study, however, could be that people do not master the content of Scripture itself.

LESSON 9

1. God is not unknowable. By His good grace He has condescended to us and revealed Himself to His creatures. However, we are finite and therefore the knowledge that we can have is not comprehensive.

2. The Latin phrase *Finitum non capax infiniti* can be translated, "the finite cannot contain the infinite" or "the infinite cannot be contained." Our minds are finite,

and our finite minds do not have the ability or the capacity to grasp all that God encompasses.

3. Univocal means "having one meaning," and it is used to describe things that are identical when applied to one being or another. Though related, we do not mean exactly the same thing when we speak of God's love and our own love. The love of God is infinitely greater. Thus, while avoiding double standards, we cannot speak univocally of God's communicable attributes.

4. Analogical means "likeness" or "similarity." Although God is not completely different from us (equivocal), He is not identical to us (univocal). To say that there is a relation between "God is good" and "my neighbor is good" is to speak analogically.

5. John Calvin says that part of the graciousness and the mercy of God is that God condescends and lisps for our benefit, by addressing us on our terms and in our own language forms—just like a parent may coo when they talk to an infant but still communicate something that is meaningful and intelligible.

6. The way of negation, or *via negationis*, is one of the more common ways we speak about God in theology. We describe God sometimes by saying what He is not. We say that God is infinite or that He is not bound by anything and that He is immutable or that He does not change.

LESSON 10

1. Despite their repeated falls into idolatry, the Old Testament clearly teaches monotheism: "the LORD is one" (Deut. 6:4). This foundational part of the Ten Commandments was the cornerstone of the Jew's religious identity.

2. What God has revealed to us concerning His triune nature is true, and we can understand and know it. However, that does not mean that there is no mystery to the Trinity.

3. John 1:1 teaches that Jesus (the *Logos*) was intimately with (*pros*) God, thus He is a distinct person in relation to God the Father, but also that the *Logos* was God, an ascription of deity to Jesus.

4. Christianity, like Judaism before it, rejects polytheism. Yet, God has revealed Himself in three distinct persons: Father, Son, and Holy Spirit. Therefore, we affirm both the oneness and the threeness of God within the Trinity.

5. *Prosōpon* describes a face-to-face relationship, which is the most intimate way in which persons relate to each other—in a face-to-face perspective of intimacy. This is the term John uses when he says, "In the beginning was the Word, and the Word

was *with* God." The word was *pros* God; the *Logos* was in this closest possible relationship to God.

6. There are many descriptive terms used for Jesus in the New Testament, but the one that dominated the thinking of the theologians in the first 300 years of the church's reflection was the concept of the *logos*. It wasn't merely because it was a difficult concept to grasp, but it provided an exalted view of the nature of Christ.

LESSON 11

1. The Trinity is a paradox, not a contradiction. God is both one and three, but not at the same time or in the same relationship. He is one in essence and three in person.

2. The word "essence" comes from the Greek word *ousia*, which has to do with being and substance. Dr. Sproul refers to its vernacular translation, which could simply mean *stuff.*

3. The word *persona* was both a legal and theatrical term. In the theater, it described the masks used to distinguish between characters that were played by one actor. Theologically, this analogy must not be taken too far, however, or we risk falling into modalism—the heretical view that the Father, Son, and Holy Spirit are only different manifestations of one person.

4. The word *existence* means "to stand out of." It connotes our derivative nature as creatures. God, on the other hand, is self-existent, and therefore does not *exist* in the strict sense.

5. Underneath the pure being of God, at a lower dimension, we distinguish among three subsistences, which the Bible calls Father, Son, and Holy Spirit. They are not three existences or three beings, but rather, three subsistences within that one eternal being that is God.

6. We can say that the distinction among the three persons is a necessary distinction because the Bible makes that distinction, but we cannot say that it is an essential distinction. When we say that the differences among the Father, Son, and the Holy Spirit are real but not essential, we are being specific and precise with respect to the word *essential*, saying these represent real differences within the godhead but not within the essence of deity itself.

LESSON 12

1. It is possible to conceive of a self-existent being which exists out of necessity. The alternative idea of self-creation is nonsensical. For anything to exist in the universe there had to have been a self-existent being from the beginning.

2. God's incommunicable attributes belong to Him alone. It would be impossible for Him to bestow these attributes on another god, for a created being cannot be eternal, infinite, self-existent, etc.

3. God's transcendence speaks of His otherness. He is infinitely greater than any of His creatures in heaven or on earth, but He is by no means absent from His creation.

4. When John Stuart Mill argued that God does not exist because God would Himself need a cause, he misapplied the law of causality. The law states that every effect must have a cause, not that everything has a cause.

5. An important principle we need to understand is that God is a simple being —not simple to understand, not simple in the sense of being simplistic or easy, but that God is not made up of parts. It is not so much that God has attributes as that He is His attributes and that He is His attributes in an undivided, simple way.

6. The difference between God and creatures is that we are human beings and God is the Supreme Being. Even though humans can be classified as beings, they are not self-existent. Humans are dependent beings while God is not dependent, not created, not finite, but has the power of being in Himself.

LESSON 13

1. Even though the quickening of the Holy Spirit gives the potential to be imitators of God, we are still creatures. When we are glorified in heaven, we will not become divine beings.

2. One of God's attributes is mercy, which is not justice per se, but is also not unjust. Even though justice and mercy are not the same thing, justice is linked to righteousness, and righteousness may, at times, include within it the idea of mercy and grace.

3. We are called to be holy (set apart, righteous) as God is holy. However, there is another use of the word *holy* which denotes God's majesty and transcendence, which is not shared with His creatures.

4. Wisdom is doing that which pleases God, and it is through His Word, that we learn what pleases Him. Wisdom is a communicable attribute, and God Himself is the fountainhead and source of all wisdom. If we lack wisdom, we are called as Christians to pray that God would illuminate our thinking; He gives us His Word that we might be wise.

5. The book of Proverbs tells us that the fear of the Lord is the beginning of wisdom. For the Jew, the very essence of wisdom biblically is found in godly living; it's not just in clever knowledge. The purpose of gaining knowledge is that we may become wise—wise in the sense of knowing how to live in a way that is pleasing to God.

6. Jesus told the rich young ruler that nobody is good except God (Mark 10:18; Luke 18:19). In our fallen condition, we do not imitate and reflect the goodness of God's character. Yet, once we are regenerated by the Holy Spirit, we are called to a life of good works, so that with the help of the Holy Spirit, we can approach the character and quality of goodness, and mirror and reflect this aspect of God's nature.

LESSON 14

1. While this Scripture passage does say that we cannot know the hidden will of God ("the secret things belong to the Lord"), it makes a point of noting that we can know the revealed will of God ("the things that are revealed belong to us and to our children").

2. The Bible frequently speaks about the determinate fore-council of God, where God decreed from all eternity that Christ should die on the cross in Jerusalem at a particular time in history (Acts 2:23). What God decrees will surely come about; His decretive will ordains everything that comes to pass.

3. When God prohibited attempts to see into the future, He was setting apart His hidden will, which is none of our business. That is why God is severe in His warnings in Scripture against those who try to find out the future through illicit means. In our day, these would be Ouija boards, fortune tellers, tarot cards, etc.

4. God's preceptive will is that which He commands and desires for us. He has revealed that to us in His law or His Word. The Christian should apply Himself to knowing God's will as written in His Word.

5. Trusting in Christ, abstaining from sexual immorality, and loving justice and mercy are all a part of the will of God for our lives. However, we find all these things in the Word of God, of which we are commanded to obey every word.

6. John Calvin said, "Where God closes His holy mouth, I will desist from inquiry." If we were to translate that into modern nomenclature, we could say something like this: "The hidden will of God is none of our business." That's why it is hidden.

LESSON 15

1. The concept of divine providence has to do with God's sovereign control over the universe. Ephesians 1:11 says that God "works all things according to the counsel of his will."

2. The Bible does not promise that we will live a life of ease, pleasure, and comfort; in fact, it tells us that the Christian life will be marked by trials and suffering. In all that comes to us, however, we know that God is working everything, both the good and bad, for His glory and our ultimate good.

3. The etymology of *providence* (beforehand/to see) has to do with foresight, but conceptually it has more to do with provision. God governs history with an eye towards His children, readying His Bride for His wedding feast.

4. One of the oldest slogans in the ancient church that sought to summarize the essence of the relationship between God and His people is the phrase <u>*Deus pro nobis*</u>—God for us. This phrase refers to the phrase in Romans 8:31 that says "If God is for us, who can be against us?"

5. The first time we meet the word for providence in the Old Testament is in the Genesis 22 in the narrative account of the attempted sacrifice of Isaac. Abraham told Isaac that God would provide a lamb for the sacrifice, and He did. The ultimate provision that God makes by virtue of His divine sovereignty is the provision of the supreme Lamb who was sacrificed on our behalf.

6. In the Old Testament, we read of God's work of creation: "In the beginning, God created the heavens and the earth" (Gen. 1:1). The Hebrew word for "create" is *bara'*. It denotes more than mere creation and conveys the idea is that God sustains and preserves what He creates and brings into being.

LESSON 16

1. The Latin phrase *ex nihilo* means "out of nothing." The Christian view of creation is not "Out of nothing, something came," but "In the beginning was God, and He alone created from nothing." He did not create the universe with existing matter, but by the power of His word He brought all things into being.

2. Though the concept of spontaneous generation has been shown to be an impossibility, renowned scientists still teach the concept under the names "gradual spontaneous generation" or "chance creation."

3. Though some may plead the case that the world is merely an illusion, most agree upon the existence of the universe. To argue nothing exists is a self-defeating argument, since you first have to exist to argue against existence.

4. Some will speak of the universe as created by random chance, but this concept ascribes being and power to chance, which is not substantial. To say the universe came into being by chance goes back to the idea of self-creation, because chance is nothing.

5. In the Enlightenment, the "lights came on," so to speak, and the existence of God was no longer considered necessary to explain the external universe. Alternatives to the God hypothesis came about through scientific advancements.

6. God's transcendence is not limited to His location; He is above and beyond the universe in His being. God has the power of being and eternal existence within Himself, therefore His transcendence is ontological.

LESSON 17

1. Materialists and skeptics such as Rudolf Bultmann want to rid the Bible of its miraculous and supernatural elements, but the Word of God unapologetically teaches the reality of the supernatural.

2. During the Middle Ages, the practice of mocking the devil led to the image of Satan with red horns and a pitchfork. The comical depiction of Satan is not biblical, but the Bible does affirm the existence of the devil.

3. The Greek word for "angel" actually appears more often in the New Testament than the words for "love" and "sin." The fact that the New Testament speaks of angels more often than love and sin means that angels should be taken seriously.

4. Controversy arose during the early church over the belief that Christ was merely an angel—a supernatural being, more than a man but less than God. Yet Hebrews teaches that Christ is above the angels as the heir of all things.

5. In Scripture, the first task of angels is to minister, and they fulfill this role in different ways. They are invisible, created spirits who manifest themselves at different times in ministering to the saints of God, but specifically to Christ during His earthly ministry.

6. Christians should not underestimate the devil, but neither should we overestimate him. Satan is the tempter, accuser, and deceiver, but he is just a creature and not the opposite power of God. Satan is stronger than us, but he is weaker than God and can be resisted by those who are in Christ. Ultimately, the devil is a vanquished foe, defeated by Christ.

LESSON 18

1. The dignity of man is based on the fact that we are created by God and our significance for existence is rooted in the *imago Dei*. Attempts to undermine the Creator ultimately rob man of his dignity as well.

2. The Latin phrase *imago Dei* refers to man's being created in the image of God. Humanity is not equal with God, but mankind bears His image and likeness.

3. Insisting that God is "wholly other," Karl Barth rejected the *analogia entis* (analogy of being), the idea that we are like God. Instead, he believed that the image of God relates to the *analogia relationis* (analogy of relationship). The problem with this

view is that in order for us to relate to God, we have to be like Him somewhat; He cannot be completely different from us.

4. The idea is that, since God has an interpersonal relationship within the Godhead, He created human beings as male and female as an analogy for the Trinity. The problem with this analogy is that animals are relational as well. Also, if the image of God does not mean we are made like God, then we cannot communicate with God.

5. Animals can think by instinct, but humans have a higher capacity for reason and are held accountable for their actions. Like God, we have power for contemplation and faculty for choosing, which is unique in the created world.

6. As image bearers of God, humans have the responsibility to mirror and reflect God's image as His representatives in creation. Sin has distorted man's ability to reflect God, but Christ, as the second Adam, was the perfect fulfillment of the *imago Dei.*

LESSON 19

1. Humankind was not the only thing affected by sin. The curse of the fall caused cosmic upheaval, and all of creation groans as it awaits restoration.

2. Because of the fall, we are estranged from God, from one another, and even from ourselves. Before becoming Christians, we "were alienated and hostile in mind, doing evil deeds" (Col. 1:21), "hostile to God" (Rom. 8:7), and "hated by others and hating one another" (Titus 3:3).

3. The word *hamartia* came from archery and had to do with missing the target. Thus, we fall short of God's standard for holiness, for "all have sinned and fall short of the glory of God" (Rom. 3:23).

4. Transgression is an active violation of God's law. We trespass God's law when we actively cross a line set by God's standard. There are sins of commission and omission: we do that which we ought not to do, and we don't do that which we ought to do.

5. The Latin terms *privatio* and *negatio,* meaning "privation" and "negation," refer to the nature of evil in negative terms. Because of sin, we lack perfect righteousness and possess the opposite of good.

6. Since evil is a negation, it cannot be understood apart from God's positive norm. The problem of evil is not an illusion; it is active and real, being against God's good.

LESSON 20

1. While Scripture better explains the nature of original sin, the evidence for it is in the pervasive evil and sin around us every day. The universality of sin is apparent everywhere and demands an explanation.

2. Though related closely to the sin of Adam and Eve in the garden, the doctrine of original sin has to do with the consequences and results of that sin. Original sin describes our sinful condition out of which we commit actual sins.

3. In the garden, man was created *posse peccare* and *posse non peccare*, that is, with the ability to sin and the ability not to sin. When Adam and Eve disobeyed God, mankind lost the ability not to sin. The only person who lived a sinless life was Jesus Christ.

4. Because of the fall, we are wholly enslaved to sin. It's not that we are unable to do what we want to do, but rather that we don't want to obey in the first place. We are not morally able to do the good that God requires.

5. Civil virtue is when we do good deeds externally without the internal motivation of love for God. We often find ourselves obeying the law but lacking the desire to obey out of love for the God of the law.

6. Because of original sin, we are unable to come to God on our own. We still have a will to make choices, but our will is enslaved to our fallen nature, which only wants to sin. We need God to do a work in us first; this work is the effectual calling of the Holy Spirit (Rom. 8:29–31).

LESSON 21

1. We don't go through our own probationary period or experience our own fall and thus condemnation. Rather, Adam's sin in the garden is transmitted to us as his descendants.

2. Original sin means that we are all sinners from birth (Ps. 51:5). On this side of the fall, no one is born without sin, except for Christ. Christ assumed a human nature that was not tainted by sin.

3. The view that the souls of all humans somehow existed at the time when Adam and Eve sinned and that we participated in the fall—thus making us directly culpable—is a crass version of realism.

4. Though the sophisticated realist view has been held by brilliant minds in church history, such as Jonathan Edwards, it is dependent on the Platonic ideals of ideas and forms that pre-exist in the mind of God.

5. The view of transmission known as federalism holds that God deals with us covenantally, and that Adam was our representative, our covenant head. We cannot escape the transfer of guilt because God chose Adam as our representative. All mankind was covenantally represented by Adam when he fell (Rom. 5:12), and it is because of this covenantal standing that we find salvation in Jesus Christ (Rom. 5:17).

6. Christ accomplished what the first representative could not. Because of one man's sin, all have sinned and fall short of the glory of God, but in Christ many are made righteous.

LESSON 22

1. A covenant is an agreement between two parties based upon a promise. The promise is made on condition that stipulations are fulfilled and oaths dramatize the reality of the covenant promise.

2. The covenant of redemption is not made with any creatures, but is a covenant made between the persons of the Godhead. From all eternity, the Father, Son, and Holy Spirit agreed to accomplish the redemption of the elect.

3. The covenant of works refers to the command God gave Adam and Eve in the garden. In a state of probation, God promised eternal life based on their performance. The destiny of the human race depended on the works of the federal head, who would procure life for his progeny if he obeyed but would procure death for his progeny if he disobeyed.

4. The very fact that God condescends to relate to His creature in covenant makes the covenant of works a gracious covenant. God is not required to promise His creation anything.

5. The promise of redemption is promised to Adam and Eve in Genesis 3:15, where God was pleased to establish a second covenant with man. In this covenant, commonly called the covenant of grace, God promises redemption to mankind through the work of Jesus Christ.

6. The covenant of works is not nullified by the covenant of grace. Rather, it is fulfilled by Christ's substitutionary work in the covenant of grace. We are saved by God's grace through faith *in the work* of Jesus Christ.

LESSON 23

1. Christology is the study of the person and work of Christ. Christology is essential for the life of a Christian, since Christ has redeemed us and revealed to us the majesty of the Father.

2. Though Jesus of Nazareth is a real historical figure, the identity of Christ is found in Scripture. In the four Gospels, Christ's character is revealed through His life and ministry as told from four distinct perspectives of His disciples.

3. In Revelation 5, Christ is portrayed as the bloodied Lamb who was slain. At the center of the heavenly throne room is the Lamb of God. This imagery describes the contrast between Christ's humiliation and His exaltation.

4. Christ is found throughout the Bible. The promise of the Messiah is given in the Old Testament, and Christ is declared the fulfillment of Old Testament prophecy by the New Testament writers. All of Scripture points to Christ.

5. Christ has two natures in His one person. He is both truly God and truly man. Both natures were necessary to accomplish the work of redemption as the only Mediator between God and man.

6. Jesus Himself declared His own divinity when He said, "Before Abraham was, I am" (John 8:58). The Greek phrase *egō eimi*, meaning "I am," is a clear allusion to the answer God gave Moses when he asked for God's name: "Say this to the people of Israel: 'I AM has sent me to you'" (Ex. 3:14).

LESSON 24

1. The mystery of the incarnation and the unity of Christ's natures are explained through what Christ is not. The creeds set boundaries and borders for orthodoxy, and to go beyond them is to land upon some heresy.

2. The Latin phrase *Deum verum et hominem verum* translates as "truly God and truly man." To be orthodox, a confession of Christ must affirm both His true humanity and His true deity.

3. In order to uphold monotheism, Eutyches suggested that Jesus has only one nature that is a mixture of the divine and human natures. He believed that, instead of two distinct natures in one person, Jesus has a third nature, which is the separate natures combined.

4. Nestorianism is the antithesis of Eutychianism. Instead of combining the two natures of Christ, it completely divides them into two separate persons: a divine Jesus and a human Jesus.

5. In Greek, the word for God is *theos* and the word for man is *anthrōpos*. Eutyches defined the theanthropic nature of Christ as neither human or divine—a blend that is partly divine and partly human, but not fully either.

6. The definition of Chalcedon follows the formula *vere homo vere Deus*, which means "truly man and truly God." With the famous four negatives, the definition describes

what Christ is not. Christ has two natures without confusion, mixture, division, or separation.

LESSON 25

1. *Christ* comes from the Greek word *Christos* which is the Greek translation of the Old Testament word *Messiah*, meaning "Anointed One." *Christ* is Jesus' most common title, but it is not His last name.

2. Though *Son of Man* ranks third in the most frequently used titles of Christ in the New Testament overall, it is the number one title Jesus used for Himself. In Daniel 7:13, the Son of Man is given authority to judge the world and represents the divine visitation of the Lord. In context, this title does not refer to Jesus' humility but to His unique authority as Messiah.

3. The Greek word translated "Lord" in the New Testament is *kurios*. Caesar ascribed this term to himself, but followers of Jesus confessed, "*Jesus ho kurios*," which means "Jesus is Lord."

4. *Lord* in small capitals is a translation of the sacred name *Yahweh*. When "Lord" is used in upper- and lowercase letters, it is a translation of the Hebrew word *Adon* or *Adonai*, the highest title for God as sovereign Creator.

5. *Doulos* in the New Testament was a term for one who was enslaved. When we declare Christ as Lord, we understand that we are not our own; we have been purchased by the blood of Christ. In Christ, we are no longer slaves to sin but slaves of Christ.

6. The imperial use of *Lord* is the highest use of the term. This meaning caused the most trouble for the early church, since Caesar claimed sole title to the imperial usage. The New Testament also says no one can call Jesus "Lord" except by the Holy Spirit, which means one can confess Christ as Lord in the imperial exalted sense and yet not be redeemed. Only those regenerated by the Spirit can make a sincere confession.

LESSON 26

1. The states of Christ do not begin at Christ's birth in Bethlehem. Before the incarnation in eternity past, Christ existed in His preincarnate state before the foundation of time (John 1:1–14).

2. A theophany is an outward manifestation of the invisible God, as with the burning bush. A Christophany is an outward manifestation of the second person of the Trinity before His birth.

3. The state of humiliation refers to Christ's emptying Himself of the glories of heaven by taking on flesh in the incarnation (Phil. 2:5–11). Throughout His life, there was a progression of deeper humiliation as He moved toward the cross.

4. Other than Christ's second coming in glory at the consummation of history, the ascension was the climax of Christ's exaltation. His ascension was more than Christ just going up to heaven. The ascension was Christ's elevation to His coronation, and He now rules on the throne as King of kings.

5. Some consider there to be a line between Christ's humiliation and exaltation; that the resurrection marked the end of His humiliation. But the exaltation of Christ actually began at the moment of His death and memorial burial before His resurrection, fulfilling the prophecy of Isaiah 53.

6. Though the incarnation brought Christ into a state of humiliation, Christ still has a physical resurrected body in His glorified state, which foreshadows the hope of the resurrection of our bodies. Christ incarnate has been raised as the firstborn of the brethren.

LESSON 27

1. The *munus triplex* or threefold office of Christ speaks of His role as Prophet, Priest, and King. As our Mediator, Christ serves all three offices in the Old Testament. As a Prophet, He speaks truth to God's people and is Truth. As Priest, Christ made the final sacrifice and intercedes for us in the heavenly temple. As King, Christ rules on the throne of God as the King of kings and Lord of lords.

2. Because God is holy and we are sinners, we need a Mediator to stand between us and God. Just as Moses interceded on behalf of the children of Israel, so Christ intercedes for us as one greater than Moses (1 Tim. 2:5).

3. Where the Old Testament prophets would distinguish between their words and God's words by the phrase "Thus saith the Lord," Jesus could say, "Truly, I say to you." Christ doesn't just speak the word of God, but He is the Word of God; He is the subject and object of prophecy.

4. As our perfect High Priest, Christ is our High Priest forever. The priesthood of Christ is higher than the priesthood of Aaron or Levi and goes back to the mysterious order of Melchizedek.

5. Like David, who learned to be a good king by shepherding sheep, Christ is our great shepherd King who is also a priestly and prophetic King. His kingdom will have no end, and He will reign forever.

6. When Jesus began His public ministry, He declared that "the time is fulfilled, and the kingdom of God is at hand" (Mark 1:15), and when He ascended into heaven, He

sat down "at the right hand of God" (Col. 3:1; see Ps. 110). Christ's first coming was the breaking in and the inauguration of His kingdom.

LESSON 28

1. *Cur Deus homo* is a Latin phrase famously used by Anselm of Canterbury, which means "Why the God-man?" This question probes the mystery of the atonement.

2. "It is finished" is a commercial statement referring to the end of a payment. Christ purchases His bride; we have been bought with the blood of Christ. Redemption comes at a very high cost.

3. One of the most popular ransom theories is that Christ paid a ransom to Satan to release His people from captivity. This theory gives more power and authority to Satan than he deserves.

4. *Christus Victor* emphasizes Christ's cosmic victory on the cross. Christ's triumph over evil is the fulfillment of the promise in Genesis 3:15. Christ crushed the head of Satan, though His victory was not without pain.

5. The satisfaction theory is based on an understanding of the holiness of God and the infinite offense that sin represents. Because we have sinned against a perfectly holy God, we deserve death. A judge who never punishes evil is not a just judge; God's justice demands that evil be punished.

6. Dr. Sproul explains pecuniary debt with the illustration of the boy in the ice cream shop. Pecuniary debt is the little boy's not having enough money for his order; moral debt is the boy's stealing his ice cream and being caught.

LESSON 29

1. *Huper* means "on behalf of." Karl Barth once remarked that *huper* was the most important word in the Bible when speaking of Christ's redemption. Redemption is accomplished for us by someone else.

2. On the Day of Atonement, the scapegoat was brought to the high priest, who transferred the sins of the people to the goat by the laying of hands, and then chased the goat outside of the camp away from the presence of God. A lamb was then slain and its blood was sprinkled on the mercy seat of the ark of the covenant. These sacrifices were shadows that pointed to Christ's authentic atonement of substitution.

3. As symbolized by the scapegoat, expiation is the removal of guilt. Propitiation is the satisfaction of the moral obligation. Both the horizontal and vertical dimensions of atonement involve a substitute. We are saved by Christ's obedient life and death.

4. We all know deep down that we are guilty before God, and the answer to that guilt is the death of Christ on our behalf. The question isn't, Why did Christ die? but, How can His death remove my guilt?

5. All of us are under the curse of sin and cut off from the blessing of God. Apart from Christ, we cannot dwell with a holy God. Christ became a curse for us so that we might be restored to the presence of God.

6. Christ graciously lavished many gifts upon us, but the blessing that Christ secured through His atoning death on the cross was access to the presence of God. Sin destroyed our relationship with God, and Christ's substitutionary work of atonement restored that relationship.

LESSON 30

1. The scope of Christ's atonement is limited. A better wording would be *definite atonement*, since the value of Christ's atonement is not limited. The atonement is sufficient, but it isn't applied to all people. Salvation is definite for the elect.

2. The doctrine of limited atonement holds that Christ atoned for the sins of His elect alone. Every person for whom Christ died is saved.

3. Christ died for a people from every tribe, tongue, and nation, but that does not mean that He died for each and every person individually. For this reason, we are called to preach the gospel to all people in every part of the world, so that God's elect from every tribe, tongue, and nation might hear the gospel and be saved.

4. Universalism is the theory that Jesus died so that everyone in the universe might be redeemed. This view maintains that everyone in the universe is saved because of the universal application of the atonement of Christ. If there is one person in hell, then universalism cannot be true.

5. Limited atonement teaches that salvation is not simply made possible by the death of Christ, but that His blood actually paid the debt of all His elect. Salvation is a completed work.

6. Though people might desire to hold to Calvinism without holding to the doctrine of limited atonement, to do so is inconsistent with the idea of unconditional election. Total depravity, unconditional election, irresistible grace, and perseverance of the saints all make limited atonement necessary.

LESSON 31

1. The first time we see the Holy Spirit is in the creation account. We read, "And the Spirit of God was hovering over the face of the waters" (Gen. 1:2).

2. The Greek word *dunamis* is translated "power" and is applied in Scripture to the Spirit. The angel Gabriel told Mary that God's Spirit and power (*dunamis*) would overshadow her and cause her to conceive (Luke 1:35).

3. The Holy Spirit anointed certain individuals in the Old Testament to the offices of prophet, priest, and king. However, not every believer had the anointing for ministry, and not every anointed leader was a believer.

4. The Holy Spirit anointed various individuals in the Old Testament. However, the outpouring of the Spirit on every believer was an event that the Old Testament anticipated would take place under the new covenant.

5. During Moses' ministry, Jethro, his father-in-law, observed Moses stretching himself thin in leading the multitude of Israel. At the suggestion of Jethro and with the approval of God, Moses separated for himself seventy men to be elders of the people and to share in the leadership.

6. The first time the Old Testament speaks of anyone as filled with the Spirit was in reference to the artists who were uniquely endowed and gifted by the Holy Spirit to do their work. The critical point is that not everyone in the camp had this gift. Moses looked forward to a new Mediator who would give His Spirit to all of His people, so that this empowerment for ministry would be given to all God's people.

LESSON 32

1. The Greek word *pneuma* and the Hebrew word *ruach* can both be translated as "wind," "breath," or "spirit." In the creation account, God breathed life into Adam, and he became a living spirit.

2. Though the work of the Spirit is connected to all the above, it is in His role as giver of life that the Spirit is involved in creation and redemption. He breathes life into all humans and new life into all true Christians.

3. Unless we are born of the Spirit, we cannot enter the kingdom (John 3:5). To be in the presence of a holy God requires that we ourselves be holy. For this, we need the sanctifying work of the Holy Spirit.

4. Jesus promised that the Holy Spirit would lead His people into all truth (John 16:13). The Holy Spirit helps us understand the Scriptures by shedding light into our minds to help us see what is in the text. This process is known as illumination.

5. One of the chief works that occurs in the New Testament is regeneration, the impartation of new life to dead souls. Regeneration is the function of God the Holy Spirit, and there is great emphasis placed upon this work in the New Testament.

6. David had to be born of the Holy Spirit; Abraham had to be born of the Holy Spirit. Everyone who's ever been redeemed had to be born of the Spirit of God in order to escape spiritual death and the flesh. Regeneration is an absolute necessity for salvation.

LESSON 33

1. Jesus tells His disciples that when He leaves He will send the Holy Spirit as "another Paraclete." Christ Himself is also a Paraclete, our advocate before the Father.

2. Though the term *comforter* has come to be associated with one who brings consolation during times of pain, the root meaning is "with strength." The primary work of the Holy Spirit is to come to strengthen God's people to be courageous in the midst of fearful tribulation.

3. The paraclete was a family lawyer who would be summoned during times of crisis. He would be an advocate for the accused against accusations.

4. Though the Holy Spirit is mentioned throughout the Bible, it is in the Upper Room Discourse that Jesus gives us insight into the person and work of the Holy Spirit, who came as another Paraclete after Jesus ascended into heaven.

5. Nietzsche was critical of Christianity's impact on Western civilization. Nietzsche abhorred what he considered the ethic of weakness propagated by Christianity and its emphasis on humility, patience, and kindness. Nietzsche called for an ethic of strength and machismo, emphasizing the ideal expressed by the image of a conqueror.

6. The Upper Room Discourse is the final teaching session that Jesus had with His disciples on the night in which He is betrayed. This important section of Scripture instructs us about the character of the Holy Spirit and His mission. It came at a time when Jesus was preparing His disciples for His imminent departure.

LESSON 34

1. Pentecostal theology originally taught a doctrine of sanctification known as "the second blessing," which signified arrival at perfection. The sign of having received that baptism of the Holy Spirit was speaking in tongues.

2. Pentecost was the promised outpouring of the Holy Spirit. Before, during the Old Testament, certain anointed men would receive the Holy Spirit. Now, all believers everywhere receive the Holy Spirit.

3. According to Dr. Sproul, there is no time gap between when a person is filled with the Holy Spirit and when he is regenerated. A new believer has the Holy Spirit immediately at conversion.

4. The outpourings of the Spirit on the Jews and the gentiles represent the expansion of the gospel, moving out to the ends of the earth. As the gospel moved out from Jerusalem, Jew and gentile alike were given the Holy Spirit.

5. Gentiles were aliens to the commonwealth of Israel and were strangers to the covenant in the Old Testament. There was partial membership given to God-fearers and absolutely no membership given to Samaritans, and gentiles were considered to be outside the camp. As the gospel was preached to these groups, the primary issue was whether they had full membership rights in the body of Christ.

6. When the seventy elders were anointed by the Holy Spirit, Joshua was worried that some of them should not be prophesying in the camp. However, Moses was not concerned and wished that God would give every member of the community His Spirit for ministry.

LESSON 35

1. Though there is no explicit teaching on this from Acts, Dr. Sproul suggests that the miracle of Pentecost was one of hearing (supernatural translation). As such, the miracle was not that people spoke in tongues, but that people were hearing different languages in their native tongue.

2. The manifestations of the gift of tongues has been far from uniform throughout the history of the church, such that there is exceedingly sparse evidence for the continuity of the gift of tongues after the first century. This challenges the assumption that Corinth's experience was normative.

3. The whole church is equipped to exercise their gifts in order to minister, serve, encourage, and edify each other. In this way, the church manifests what the Reformers called "the priesthood of all believers."

4. Speaking in tongues builds up the individual, but prophesying builds up the church. That is why Paul tells us, "I want you all to speak in tongues, but even more to prophesy" (1 Cor.14:5).

5. Paul teaches that gifts are pointless if they are not practiced in love. The Apostle makes it abundantly clear that the gift of love is far more important to the people of God than spectacular gifts.

6. When Paul is encouraging people to prophesy, he is referring to the ability to articulate the truth of God. This can be observed when a preacher preaches or when a Christian verbally bears witness to his faith.

LESSON 36

1. It is possible to be gifted but immature. God calls us to grow up in Christ and to put away lesser things. The solution to immaturity is to cultivate the fruit of the Holy Spirit in one's life.

2. When Paul discusses the "works of the flesh" (Gal. 5:19), he uses the Greek word *sarx*. This word is often used in reference to sinful flesh as a metaphysical reality.

3. Though meekness is often confused with weakness, true meekness is having power but choosing graciousness. Jesus was the perfect embodiment of this fruit.

4. We are God's people, and we will either please or grieve the Holy Spirit by how we live. If we aren't to grieve the Holy Spirit, we must bear fruit in keeping with repentance.

5. The first Apostolic mandate for Christian people is that we are to walk in the Spirit. This does not mean that our primary task is to pursue mysticism or to be caught up in shortcuts to spirituality. The demonstration of our walk in the Spirit is manifested by the fruit of the Spirit.

6. The fruits of the Spirit imitate the character of God. God is long-suffering in that He is slow to anger and not hasty to judge, but He is patient and forbearing, giving His people time to repent. In this way, long-suffering is related to patience.

LESSON 37

1. Even though the word *miracle* appears in English translations, there is no direct Greek or Hebrew word that corresponds to it. The New Testament uses words for signs, wonders, and powers to represent what we call miraculous.

2. Whenever there is an explosion of miraculous activity in Scripture, it is to prove that the claimed revelation is truly from God. One of the reasons we believe Scripture is a truly divine revelation is because its authors and their messages were authenticated by miracles from God.

3. The Apostle Paul says that Jesus "was declared to be the Son of God in power according to the Spirit of holiness by his resurrection from the dead" (Rom. 1:4). The resurrection of Jesus Christ vindicates His claims of divinity.

4. Though he has power to deceive and may do false miracles, the truly miraculous is beyond his grasp because Satan is not God. Only the Creator of all things has the power to perform the miraculous.

5. A miracle is an extraordinary work performed by the immediate power of God in the external perceivable world. It is an act against nature that only God can do, such

as bringing life out of death or something out of nothing. This narrow definition provides parameters when discussing the nature of miracles.

6. The Reformers did not tell the Roman critics that their understanding of the function of miracles was wrong; they understood the significance of miracles. The Reformers claimed that they did have miracles that proved their teaching, and that they were recorded in the New Testament. The authority of the Apostles is proved by miracles, which establishes the trustworthiness of Scripture.

LESSON 38

1. *Soteriology* is not a word commonly used in the church, but it is an important word because it's deals with those matters that pertain to salvation. The branch of theology known as soteriology is the study of the message of salvation as taught in Scripture.

2. By definition, grace is unmerited favor and therefore not obligatory. God was not required to show grace to anyone, but He did because of His own voluntary, good, and merciful will.

3. Theological liberals deny the special grace of revelation by focusing solely on common grace matters, such as care for the poor. Both special grace and common grace are gifts from God to which we must be faithful to attend.

4. God's benevolent love is His concern for mankind. This is demonstrated in that He causes the sun to shine on the just and the unjust. This is different from His special love for His covenant people.

5. The life expectancy of the human race grew when the Christian community was faithful to God's mandate to steward His resources. Science, hospitals, and orphanages blossomed under the oversight of committed Christians.

6. God's love of complacency has to do with His redemptive love. This love is focused chiefly on His beloved Son and spills over to those who are in union with Him.

LESSON 39

1. The concept of election is found in Ephesians 1:4: "... even as he chose us in him before the foundation of the world."

2. According to Titus 3:5, "He saved us, not because of works done by us in righteousness, but according to his own mercy."

3. The prescient view of predestination understands God as looking into the future and seeing who would respond to the gospel. In this view, He then chooses them based on their faith.

4. The prescient view holds that God's decree is based on man's free decision. There can be no accusation of injustice against God if one maintains this view of election.

5. The doctrine of reprobation seeks to understand whether God has predestined some for condemnation. The question follows: If from all eternity God decrees that some are elected to salvation, does that mean that there are some who are from all eternity elected to damnation?

6. It's only when you conceive of predestination as being rooted in the sovereign good pleasure of God that people raise questions about His righteousness. Paul anticipates immediately this objection and reminds us that predestination is not a new teaching: "For he says to Moses, 'I will have mercy on whomever I will have mercy and I will have compassion on whomever I will have compassion'" (Rom. 9:15). It is God's sovereign, divine prerogative to dispense His grace and mercy however He chooses.

LESSON 40

1. *Monergism* is a compound of two Greek words: *mono*, which means "only" or "one," and *ergon*, which means "work." The Bible presents salvation as a monergistic work of God.

2. Though many theologies present this view, the Reformed view is that regeneration must precede faith. We are spiritually dead and therefore cannot respond to the gospel in faith until we have been given new life.

3. Lazarus was dead. He could do nothing until Christ raised him from the dead. After Jesus raised him, only then could he walk out of the tomb.

4. Romans 8:28–30 teaches that all those whom God effectually calls are guaranteed to be glorified. This means that God's grace cannot be thwarted in its purpose; in that sense, it is irresistible.

5. Imagine God were to ask you, "Are you worthy to be saved?" If you were to answer, "Yes, I am worthy to be saved," you would ultimately be implying that you are more righteous than others who are unworthy. This is the implication of someone who believes they merit salvation.

6. In Romans 8, Paul talks about those who are called as also being justified. The effectual call of the Holy Spirit brings about what God has designed to do from the foundation of the world. All who are predestined will be called by the Holy Spirit, all who are called by the Holy Spirit will be justified, and all who are justified will be glorified.

LESSON 41

1. When we say that justification is by faith alone, we mean that faith is the sole instrumental cause for justification—it is the hand by which we take hold of Christ. Without faith, we cannot take hold of Christ or His benefits.

2. This was the criticism of the Roman Catholic Church against Martin Luther and the Reformers who taught justification by faith alone. However, because we are declared righteous by God on the basis of Christ's merit, we may accurately refer to believers as justified sinners.

3. At the root of the Reformation conflict was the difference between imputation and infusion. Are we justified on the basis of our own infused righteousness or on the basis of the imputed righteousness of Christ? The Reformers insisted on the imputation of the perfect obedience of Christ.

4. Rome has two instrumental causes of justification. Initially, it's the sacrament of baptism, but if one loses the grace of justification then the sacrament of penance is needed to regain it. This view is in contrast to the Protestant view that faith is the only instrumental cause of justification.

5. As affirmed by the Roman Catholic Church, mortal sin is serious enough to kill the justifying grace that is possessed in the soul. If a person commits a mortal sin, he loses the grace of justification. However, one can still be restored to a state of justification through the Roman Catholic sacrament of penance.

6. Double imputation, or a double transfer, best explains the process of justification. God credits our sin to Christ and God credits Christ's righteousness to us.

LESSON 42

1. The Roman Catholic view of justification maintains that faith is necessary but works are also required (faith + works = justification). The antinomian view maintains that faith leads to justification without works (faith = justification - works), but the Reformed view maintains that faith alone leads to justification, which is accompanied by works (faith = justification + works).

2. The Latin phrase *fides viva,* which means "a living faith," was used by Martin Luther to combat those who taught that faith does not have to produce works. The Apostle James labels faith that is void of any works as a dead faith.

3. The elements of faith are *notitia* (knowledge or content of faith), *assensus* (assent to or affirmation of the content), and *fiducia* (trust in God). All three of these make up the definition of saving faith.

4. While our being made alive in Christ (regeneration) is a monergistic work of God alone, the process of conversion, whereby we repent and turn to Christ, is synergistic. When we are converted, our minds are changed dramatically.

5. The first fruit of justification is peace with God. God has declared a peace treaty with all of those who put their faith in Christ. That peace is an eternal peace, a lasting peace, an unbreakable peace, because it has been won by the perfect righteousness of Christ.

6. When God declares us just in Jesus Christ, He adopts us into His household. His only true Son is Christ, but Christ becomes our elder brother by way of adoption. When we rely on Christ for salvation, God not only declares us just but He also declares us His sons and daughters by way of adoption.

LESSON 43

1. In his book *What Is Christianity?*, Adolf von Harnack argued for the idea of the universal fatherhood of God. However, only those who have been adopted into God's family through Christ have "the right to become children of God" (John 1:12).

2. In the Lord's Prayer, Jesus taught His disciples to pray, saying, "Our Father. . . ." This wasn't an honor given to just a select few of Christ's disciples; it is part of what it means to be in God's household.

3. Those who have the Holy Spirit are being conformed to the image of Christ, the Son of God. They have been truly adopted into God's family. However, Christ is God the Son, the second person of the Trinity from all eternity. His sonship is entirely inimitable.

4. While *eis* (into) describes a transition from outside to inside, *en* (in) describes our status "in Christ," which is our mystical union with Him. We are in Christ and Christ is in us; there is a spiritual union between every Christian and Christ Himself.

5. Jewish people would address God in prayer by many titles, but "Father" was not one of them. The first reference to a Jewish person addressing God as Father was in the tenth century in Italy. No wonder it was a shock to Jesus' contemporaries when He called God "Father."

6. The idea of Christ's sonship is central to the New Testament. Not only was it radical that Jesus addressed God as Father, but there are three references in the New Testament wherein God is heard to speak audibly from heaven. In all three of those occasions, what God declares from heaven is the sonship of Jesus.

LESSON 44

1. Sanctification is a process. In this life, we are partially sanctified as we are being sanctified daily. God is constantly conforming us to the image of His Son, and He will continue to do so until we see Him face-to-face. Only then will we be fully sanctified.

2. Though perfection is not attainable this side of eternity, all true Christians bear fruit. Carnal Christianity—faith without sanctification—is a contradiction in terms.

3. Quietism is the view that sanctification is a monergistic work of God alone, and that we do not contribute anything to our sanctification.

4. We cannot add to the law where God has not spoken (contrary to the legalist) and we cannot ignore God's commands where He has clearly spoken (contrary to the antinomian).

5. The godly person, though he understands he is no longer in bondage to the law, still loves the law of God and meditates on it day and night. This is because he discovers what is pleasing to God and what reflects His character in the law.

6. Activism is the heresy of self-righteousness where sanctification is seen as something that people achieve in themselves, by themselves. This is a "pull yourself up by the bootstraps" spiritual mentality that is not aided by the grace of God.

LESSON 45

1. The parable of the sower teaches that people can receive the gospel, but without true faith, they fall away. However, those with saving faith (the good soil) produce fruit in their Christian walk.

2. According to Roman Catholic theology, mortal sins are deadly sins (e.g., murder) that destroy our status as justified before God. In order to regain our good standing, we must perform penance; however, if someone dies with a mortal sin on his record, he has lost salvation.

3. On various occasions, the authors of the New Testament addressed early Christian heresies in their writings. Whereas we do not know significant details about the book of Hebrews, such as who wrote the letter, it is likely that the author is addressing the heresy of the Judaizers. This was a group who believed that certain aspects of the Mosaic law were still binding upon Christians, particularly circumcision.

4. The author of Hebrews seems to be using the argument of the Judaizers against themselves. Since they are repudiating the finished work of Christ, they are also repudiating their salvation and hope of perseverance. As verse 9 suggests, the author is employing a "manner of speaking."

5. True believers throughout Scripture, from David to Peter, have fallen seriously. Yet, the gracious promises of God ensure that a true believer will never have a fall akin to Judas, which was full and final.

6. The only reason we can persevere is because God preserves us. If we were left to ourselves, we could fall at any moment, but our confidence rests in the promises of God to finish what He has started and rests on the efficacy of our Great High Priest who intercedes for us every day. He will preserve us.

LESSON 46

1. The English word *church* is derived from the Greek word *kuriache*, which literally means "those who are possessed or owned by the Lord." As the possessive form of the Greek word for "Lord," *kuriache* represents all of those for whom the Lord died and gathered for Himself.

2. The term *ecclesiastical* is derived from the Greek word *ekklēsia*, which is a combination of the prefix *ek* (out of) and root *kaleō* (to call). Essentially, the *ekklēsia* or church refers to the "the called-out ones."

3. The Latin phrase *corpus per mixtum* means "a mixed body." Jesus acknowledged the reality of the wheat among the tares when He said, "This people honors me with their lips, but their hearts are far from me."

4. The invisible church consists of those true believers found within the visible church. The visible church and invisible church are distinct but not separate spheres. There is overlap between the two groups.

5. Ultimately, the reason a member is excommunicated from the church is for their lack of repentance or regret for their sin. In order to bring the impenitent person to repentance, he is removed from the fellowship of the church and regarded as an unbeliever, all in the hope of restoration.

6. The church is made up of those who have true saving faith, which is why it is possible, albeit not ordinary, to be a member of the invisible church while not part of a geniune visible church.

LESSON 47

1. The building imagery of the New Testament does not limit the gospel to a brick-and-mortar building but rather refers to the nature of the church as built upon the foundation of the Apostles and prophets. Though the foundation is laid in Christ, who is the cornerstone, the chief metaphor for the foundation of the church is the Apostles and prophets.

2. The fragmentation and disintegration of the visible church into various denominations is considered by some to be the great scandal of the church. The different denominations give the impression of disunity and seem to go against what Jesus taught, which is that the church is one. Though the multiplicity of denominations can be confusing, diversity within the visible church does not mean there is no unity within the invisible church.

3. The visible church is not perfect. Disunity is due to sin and error, but the invisible church is always perfectly united in Christ. The invisible church is one while the visible church is many.

4. *Communio sanctorum* is the phrase in the Apostles' Creed that states, "I believe in the communion of the saints." Across denominational lines, there is genuine unity in the invisible fellowship found in the communion of saints. To be in Christ is to be spiritually united as part of the community of saints.

5. Biblically speaking, to be holy means to be set apart by God for a purpose. The church is holy because it is the only institution consecrated for a sacred mission and holy task that will not fail.

6. The church is holy because it is made up of people who are indwelt by God the Holy Spirit, those who have been set apart to be sanctified by the Holy Spirit Himself. It is because of the Holy Spirit that, despite human corruption, the church can rightly be called holy.

LESSON 48

1. Over time, *Roman Catholic* has been shortened to *Catholic*, but little-*c* "catholic" in the Apostles' Creed refers to the invisible, universal nature of the church. The universal church of Jesus Christ extends to all peoples around the world.

2. An Apostle was given primary authority by Christ in the early church. The office of Apostle was established by Christ as the unique transfer of His authority toward the end of His ministry to a select group of disciples. Except for the Apostle Paul, all Apostles were first disciples, but not all disciples were Apostles.

3. In the Greek, *apostolos* means "one who is sent." In ancient Greek culture, an apostle would be sent by a king as his spokesman and carried the delegated authority of the king.

4. Apostolic authority is the foundation on which the church is built. It is the line of authoritative succession from Christ to the Apostles. To reject Apostolic authority is to reject Christ, the supreme Apostle.

5. The Reformers argued you cannot have a true church if the gospel is not upheld and proclaimed. If a church denies any essential points of the gospel, that institution is no longer a church.

6. The purpose of discipline is the spiritual nurture of the church and requires some form of church government. Without church government, the practice of church discipline would not be possible.

LESSON 49

1. The great purpose for which we were created is the worship of God, and it is that purpose from which we depart in our fallen nature. Once the Holy Spirit regenerates the heart, we are able to rightly express our desire to worship.

2. Only God is worthy of worship. In worship, we honor God as God. Man, in his fallen state, refuses to worship God and give Him the honor that He is due.

3. When we don't worship God, we exchange the glory of God for a lie and worship the creature rather than the Creator. God demands that His creatures worship Him exclusively.

4. In the Old Testament, worship was seen as the giving of sacrifices. Even before sin offerings were instituted by God, there was a practice of offering of sacrifices to honor God. Though Christ has fulfilled the sacrificial system, we devote our lives to God as living sacrifices.

5. We may call someone adorable or claim to adore someone, but only God should be adored in the proper sense because adoration is worshipful love.

6. According to Jesus, proper worship is given in spirit and in truth. God wants people who will worship Him from deep within their souls.

LESSON 50

1. Baptism and the Lord's Supper are known as sacraments because they are holy and sacred gifts given by Christ to the church. In the history of the church, there has been great controversy over the administration of the sacraments because they are of great importance.

2. The historic debate over the sacraments has to do not with mode but with the number of sacraments. The Roman Catholic Church teaches that there are seven sacraments, while Protestants teach that there are two. The Reformers understood that Christ directly instituted only two sacraments: baptism and the Lord's Supper.

3. Much of the controversy of the sixteenth century concerned the sacraments. Behind the issue of justification was the debate over the function of the sacrament of penance.

4. In the Roman Catholic Church, this formula, which literally means "through the working of the works," applies to all the sacraments. It means that the sacraments communicate their benefits to all who receive them. The Reformers rejected this mode of operation and instead declared *ex opere operantis*, which means that the benefits of the sacraments are communicated only to those who receive them by faith.

5. In the Roman Catholic Church, baptism is the infusion of grace and indelible mark made upon the soul. In the Roman Catholic sacramental system, this mark is only applied once, and if lost, it can only be restored through penance.

6. In his book *The Babylonian Captivity of the Church*, Luther lashed out against the entire Roman Catholic sacramental system, which is known as sacerdotalism. In the Roman Catholic sacramental system, salvation was communicated not by faith, but through the sacraments, making the Roman Catholic Church the sole agent of salvation.

LESSON 51

1. The baptism that John the Baptist inaugurated was for the people of the Jewish nation to cleanse themselves in preparation for the coming Messiah. Christ instituted baptism as the outward sign of all the benefits we receive from Christ in the new covenant.

2. In the intertestamental period, the practice of proselyte baptism was a purification rite reserved for gentiles who wanted to become Jews because they were considered ceremonially unclean. When John the Baptist told the Jews to repent and be baptized, he was calling them unclean along with the gentiles.

3. In the old covenant, a believer had to be circumcised to be part of the community of faith. In the new covenant, Christ instituted baptism as the new sign and seal replacing circumcision as the outward sign of inclusion. There is continuity between the two covenants, but the sign of the covenant is no longer identified with Israel. The sign now signifies Christ's new covenant, where circumcision of the flesh is replaced by the circumcision of the heart.

4. In circumcision, if a person did not keep the covenant they were to be cut off from God. On the cross, Christ fulfilled the negative sanctions of circumcision by becoming a curse for us (2 Cor. 5:21).

5. Being baptized does not guarantee salvation. The benefits symbolized in baptism are actualized only when united with faith.

6. As followers of Christ, we identify with our crucified Lord through baptism, which is symbolic of His death and resurrection. The rite of baptism signifies our participation in His death and resurrection and communicates the certainty of the promises of God.

LESSON 52

1. The historical period of the New Testament did not begin until a new covenant agreement had been inaugurated. In the upper room, Christ announced the inauguration of the new covenant and instituted the Lord's Supper.

2. While celebrating the Passover with His disciples, Jesus changed the liturgy and significance of Old Testament Passover. In the Old Testament, the Passover meal was done in remembrance of Israel's deliverance from Egypt. Jesus instituted the Lord's Supper at His last Passover meal because He is the true deliverance to which the Passover had always pointed.

3. The Roman Catholic Church holds to transubstantiation. According to this view, during the Mass, the substance of the ordinary elements of bread and wine are transformed into the essence of the body and blood of Christ.

4. According to Aristotle, a thing is made up of its essence, or substance, and external perceivable qualities known as accidents. When we observe an object, we describe how it appears to our senses, but we cannot see its innermost being, its substance. According to the Roman Catholic Church, in the Mass, the substance of the bread and wine is changed into the body and blood of Christ while the accidents of bread and wine remain the same.

5. Luther argued that Christ is physically present "in, with, and under" the elements. In the Lutheran view of consubstantiation, there is a physical presence of Christ in the elements of the Lord's Supper.

6. For the Reformers, the issue of the Lord's Supper had to do with Christology, how the divine and human natures of Christ are present in the elements. Everyone agreed that Christ is present in the Lord's Supper; however, there was disagreement with regard to the mode and manner in which Christ is present.

LESSON 53

1. In Greek, *eschaton* refers to the last things or the future things that are yet to take place. Eschatology, then, is the subdivision in theology that deals with our future hope of redemption.

2. Death was never part of God's original plan for creation. The Christian understands death is part of the fallen order of things and not the original state of man. Death came into the world as God's judgment for sin.

3. Though Adam and Eve did not die immediately upon their disobedience, their sin did bring about the curse of spiritual and biological death for all mankind. God could have destroyed humanity immediately, but He granted Adam and Eve a life extension before they would experience the consequences of their sin.

4. From the Christian perspective, death is no longer a punishment for sin because Christ paid the penalty for sin on the cross. Instead, death is a moment of transition from this world to the next.

5. Paul was devoted to serving Christ but knew that death would mean being in the presence of the Lord, which is why he could say, "To live is Christ, and to die is gain" (Phil. 1:21). For Paul, life in Christ is a good thing, but departing to be with Christ is the difference between what is good and what is far better.

6. In the life of the Christian, the period between death and the resurrection is known as the intermediate state, though this is not to be confused with the heretical view of soul sleep. According to this theory, believers are separated from Christ during the intermediate state and remain unconscious and unaware of the passing of time.

LESSON 54

1. In the Greek, resurrection means "to rise again." The resurrection of the body looks forward to the rising of the body, not just a continuation of the soul after death.

2. Christ is the firstfruits of the resurrection from the dead. It is not an isolated event, but the first of many to come. The same Spirit who raised Christ from the dead will also raise our mortal bodies from the dead.

3. Christ was the first person to be resurrected from the dead because He didn't have to die again. Those whom Christ brought back to life died again, but Christ's body was transformed after His resurrection.

4. As the first person to experience the transformation of the resurrection, Christ's human body had radically changed. It was the same body that had died and been buried, but it had been glorified.

5. Christianity without the resurrection of Christ is dead. If Christ did not conquer death on the cross, there is no Christian faith, and Christians are to be pitied for placing their hope in a hoax.

6. Though our heavenly bodies will be different from our earthly bodies, we will still have human bodies. There is both continuity and discontinuity between the seed of our bodies and our future bodies.

LESSON 55

1. The expression "till kingdom come" is a reference to the Lord's Prayer, which states, "Thy kingdom come, thy will be done, on earth as it is in heaven." This petition indicates that the kingdom of God is clearly manifest in heaven, that the will of God is done every moment in heaven.

2. The one unifying theme that ties together the Bible is the kingdom of God. Early in Scripture, a promise is made of a future kingdom that will be eternal and universal. God sovereignly reigns over all creation now, but the kingdom of God is the voluntary submission of a rebellious creation to the lordship of God.

3. Though the kingdom of God awaits future consummation, the coming of Christ was the inauguration of the kingdom. John the Baptist warned, "The kingdom of God is at hand," and Jesus said, "The kingdom of God is in your midst." The King of the kingdom had arrived.

4. John the Baptist lived a life of radical self-denial while Jesus was accused of being a glutton and drunkard. Many wondered why Jesus' disciples weren't fasting as John's were, but Christ explained that it is inappropriate to fast while the bridegroom is present. The coming of Christ was a cause for celebration.

5. When the disciples asked Jesus, "Will you now restore the kingdom to Israel?" (Acts 1:6), Christ responded by commanding them to be His witnesses. Christ ascended to His heavenly coronation, but it is the job of the church to make the invisible kingdom visible, to give testimony to Christ's kingship. The King reigns now even if men are blind to His kingship, but the day is coming when every knee will bow and every tongue will confess that Jesus Christ is Lord.

6. The number one theme of the parables is the kingdom of God. The parable of the mustard seed and the parable of the leaven explain how the kingdom of God will start small and expand over time until it encompasses all things.

LESSON 56

1. The millennium, the thousand-year reign of Christ found in Revelation 20, is the most highly debated topic of eschatology. With respect to the millennium, the basic issue has to do with the question of its actual nature and its timing in relation to the second coming of Christ.

2. Since there are different views regarding the order of the millennium, the prefixes *pre*, *a*, and *post* have to do with the understanding of when the millennium occurs. The prefixes are attached to the word *millennium*.

3. Literal interpretation interprets Scripture according to its genre. If a passage is written in a poetic style, it is to be interpreted as poetry. Literalism is not to be confused with a wooden, literalistic approach that ignores genre.

4. Since Revelation is highly imaginative and filled with difficult symbols, the problem a reader faces has to do with the question of its genre and consequently what rules to apply to the book. According to the Reformers, the responsible interpreter will always interpret Scripture in the manner that it was written.

5. Premillennialism teaches there will be a literal earthly kingdom that will begin when Christ returns that establishes the beginning of the millennium. The two forms of premillennialism are historic premillennialism and dispensational premillennialism. The latter position constitutes a complete system of doctrine.

6. The scheme of dispensationalism understands Old Testament prophecies concerning Israel to have a literal future fulfillment that entails a reassembly of the Jewish state, a rebuilding of the temple, and a reinstitution of the sacrificial system. Because of these factors, only dispensationalism teaches that God has two separate plans of redemption, one for Israel and one for the church.

LESSON 57

1. The promised return of Christ to this world has been understood by the church to be the blessed hope of the people of God. The timing of Christ's return and the manner in which He will come is cause for much debate and controversy, though there is overall agreement that Christ will return as He promised.

2. According to Scripture, Christ will return personally, visibly, and in glory. Christ departed visibly and in glory at His ascension, so He will return in the same manner.

3. Realized eschatology teaches that the prophecies concerning events that accompany the return of Christ were fulfilled in the first century. This view states that all the predictions Christ made about the temple and Jerusalem were fulfilled in Christ's lifetime.

4. The destruction of the temple and the destruction of Jerusalem occurred in the first century. Christ made these predictions forty years before these events took place in AD 70.

5. A single generation in Jewish terms was forty years. When Christ made predictions about the future, He was not saying that He would return within the first generation of Christians. Rather, He was referring to the destruction of the temple and the judgement of Israel forty years later, which was within a single human generation.

6. Preterists argue that Christ returned in AD 70 in judgment on Jerusalem, though it was an invisible return. According to this view, future prophecy has already been fulfilled.

LESSON 58

1. In the nineteenth century, German philosopher Friedrich Nietzsche announced the supposed death of God. This announcement was welcomed as a victory for humanism, which believed man no longer needed reliance on a supernatural deity to improve the conditions of humanity.

2. The positivist movement of the nineteenth century was developed by Auguste Comte, who divided history into infancy, adolescence, and adulthood. The infancy stage was when people defined their lives according to religion, then grew into adolescence when they replaced religion with philosophy, but they only entered adulthood when they came to the age of science. This idea led to an optimistic view of science.

3. Along with the optimism of modernist movements in the nineteenth century came the belief that man was no longer accountable to God. Without the belief in God, people believed they no longer needed to fear a final judgment, but a life without accountability makes life meaningless. Deep down, everyone knows they are ultimately accountable for their actions, because they cannot ultimately deny God.

4. Immanuel Kant maintained that every human being has a sense of "oughtness" built into his conscience that drives ethics. He believed that there can be no meaningful ethic without this sense.

5. Jesus warned people about the coming day of judgment, but the concept is rooted in the Old Testament. In this world, justice does not always prevail, but justice will be served in the final judgment.

6. Though we are redeemed by faith, that does not mean our works count for nothing. Our works don't get us into heaven, but they will be considered at the final judgment when rewards will be distributed according to our degree of obedience.

LESSON 59

1. God does not punish innocent people, but no one is innocent. In Romans 1, Paul explains that God has revealed Himself in creation, so no man is without excuse.

2. While the person who has never heard the gospel will not be judged for rejecting the gospel, he will be judged according to the light of revelation, which he has received. Romans 1:20 reveals that all men have received sufficient knowledge of God, such that they are without excuse, for what can be known about God is made plain in the things that have been made.

3. Almost all of the biblical teaching about hell comes from the lips of Christ. If hell did not exist, Jesus would not teach on it.

4. Most language in Scripture speaks of hell as a lake of fire. Though this language may be merely symbolic, the reality is that hell is eternal separation from the grace of God. God's wrath is a consuming fire.

5. We aren't saved merely from our sin; we are saved from the wrath of God. Since God is a just God, sin cannot remain unpunished. Christ endured the wrath of God that we deserved, so that His justice would be satisfied for all those who believe.

6. According to the heretical doctrine of annihilationism, the soul of the wicked is annihilated. The loss of life is their punishment. Historically, the church has taught that the punishment of hell is conscience and eternal. If the wicked cease to exist after death, then there would be no need for hell.

LESSON 60

1. The seventh day of rest points to our future eternal rest in heaven. We will experience eternal Sabbath rest in the new heavens and the new earth.

2. Of the many reasons that Jesus gave His disciples to rejoice that He was returning to the Father, Jesus assured them that one of the reasons He was going was to prepare a place for them in His Father's house. For a believer about to enter his final rest through death, this promise is a great comfort.

3. The beatific vision is the *visio Dei*, the vision of God. It is the experience that we read about in 1 John 3:3, that "when he appears we shall be like him, because we shall see him as he is." In this lecture, Dr. Sproul asserted that this is possibly the most important eschatological text in the entire New Testament.

4. Our sight is mediated sight. Our eyes require light and external images in order that we might see. Without these things, we would not be able to see. Jonathan Edwards believed that, in heaven, we will be in such a state that our souls, without the help of our eyes, will have a direct, immediate vision of God.

5. The concept that is directly tied to the beatific vision is blessedness. Dr. Sproul connected the idea of the fulfillment we will have when we see God with ultimate blessedness. The very word *beatific* means "blissfully happy" and can be recognized in the pronouncements of blessing with which Jesus opens the Sermon on the Mount, known as the Beatitudes.

6. In Hebrew poetry, the sea is symbolic of violence. The sea is used in this negative sense because it was the source of violent weather and attack from enemies. To say there is no sea in heaven is to say there is no violence or catastrophe.